Cambridge English

OFFICIAL

MINDSET
FOR IELTS

An Official Cambridge IELTS Course

TEACHER'S BOOK 1

Cambridge University Press
www.cambridge.org/elt
Cambridge English Language Assessment
www.cambridgeenglish.org

Cambridge University Press is part of the University of Cambridge.

It furthers the University's mission by disseminating knowledge in the pursuit of
education, learning and research at the highest international levels of excellence.

www.cambridge.org
Information on this title: www.cambridge.org/9781316640111

© Cambridge University Press and UCLES 2017

First published 2017
20 19 18 17 16 15 14 13 12 11 10 9 8 7 6 5 4 3 2 1

Printed in Dubai by Oriental Press

A catalogue record for this publication is available from the British Library

Additional resources for this publication at **www.cambridge.org/mindset**

About the author

Claire Wijayatilake

Claire has been teaching English since 1988. She spent much of her career in Sri Lanka, including 16 years at British Council, Colombo. She became an IELTS Examiner in 1990 and examined regularly in Colombo and Malé, Maldives for almost 20 years. She worked as the IELTS Examiner Trainer for Sri Lanka, recruiting, training and monitoring examiners. She then moved into training and school leadership, serving as Teacher Trainer and Principal at various international schools. She returned to the UK in 2013 and worked for Middlesex University, where she started her materials writing career. She is currently a Visiting Lecturer at Westminster University, which allows her time to write. She has a PhD in Applied Linguistics and English Language Teaching from the University of Warwick.

The authors and publishers would like to thank the following people for their work on this level of the Student's Book.

Bryan Stephenson and Jock Graham for their editing and proof reading.

Design and typeset by emc design.

Audio produced by Leon Chambers at The Soundhouse Studios, London.

The publishers would like to thank the following people for their input and work on the digital materials that accompany this level.

Dr Peter Crosthwaite; Jeremy Day; Natasha de Souza; Ian Felce; Amanda French; Marc Loewenthal; Rebecca Marsden; Kate O'Toole; Emina Tuzovic; Andrew Reid; N.M.White.

Cover and text design concept: Juice Creative Ltd.

Typesetting: emc design Ltd.

Cover illustration: MaryliaDesign/iStock/Getty Images Plus.

CONTENTS

Student's Book

Mindset for IELTS Level 1 is aimed at students who are at B1 level and want to achieve a Band 5 or 5.5 result at IELTS. You can follow the book by topic and teach it lineally or alternatively you can focus on the different skills and papers that you would like your students to improve. It is designed for up to 90 hours of classroom use, but you can also focus on key areas of your choice. The topics have been chosen based on common themes in the IELTS exam and the language and skills development is based on research in the corpus, by looking at the mistakes that students at this level commonly make in IELTS.

Mindset for IELTS Level 1 offers a flexible way of teaching. You can work through the units consecutively or choose the lessons that are important to your students. You can choose to teach the book by topic or by skill.

- Topics have been chosen to suit the needs and abilities of students at this level, they are topics that occur in the IELTS exam, but are tailored to the needs and interests of your students.
- There is full coverage of the test both here and in the online modules. However, there is an emphasis on the parts of the exam where students aiming at a Band 5 or Band 5.5 will be able to pick up the most marks, maximising their chances of getting the score that they need.
- Each level of Mindset is challenging, but doesn't push students above what they can do.
- Grammar and vocabulary is built into the development of skills, so students improve their language skills as well as the skills that they need to learn to achieve the desired band score.

How *Mindset for IELTS* helps with each skill

- **Speaking** – *Mindset* gives you strategies for what happens if you don't know much of the topic. It also helps build vocabulary for each part of the test and allows students to grow in confidence.
- **Writing** – *Mindset* gives you tips on how to plan better and develop your ideas. There is coverage of all types of Task 1 and Task 2 and detailed help on how to approach each as well as model answers.
- **Reading** – Strategies for dealing with Reading texts on difficult and unknown topics are developed, as well as coverage of all question types. Strategies for improving reading skills in general as well as skills needed in the exam, such as an awareness of distraction and the use of paraphrases.
- **Listening** – *Mindset* gives coverage of all the Listening tasks, but concentrates on how your students can maximise their score. Vital skills for dealing with the paper like paraphrasing are developed and listening strategies that will help your students in everyday life are developed.

Outcomes

At the start of every lesson you will see a list of outcomes.

READING

IN THIS UNIT YOU WILL LEARN HOW TO

- respond to sentence completion questions
- skim read a text
- recognise paraphrase
- practise using the present simple and past simple.

In the Teacher's Book you will see how these outcomes relate to the lesson and the skills that your students need to develop in order to be successful in developing their English language and exam skills. There are typically three or four outcomes per lesson and look at skills that can be used both in the IELTS test and in their broader English language development; an IELTS strategy for dealing with a particular paper and a linguistic outcome that helps with vocabulary and grammar development.

Tip Boxes and Bullet Boxes

- Tip boxes help you and your students improve task awareness and language skills. You will find further information on how to get the most out of them in the Teacher's Book. Note that the number in the corner relates to the exercise that the tip goes with.

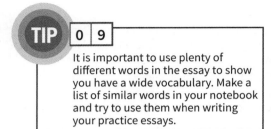

TIP 0 9

It is important to use plenty of different words in the essay to show you have a wide vocabulary. Make a list of similar words in your notebook and try to use them when writing your practice essays.

- Bullet boxes tell you how the test works and how to get a better understanding of the test task being addressed.

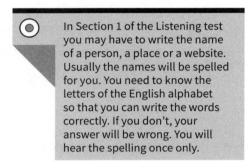

In Section 1 of the Listening test you may have to write the name of a person, a place or a website. Usually the names will be spelled for you. You need to know the letters of the English alphabet so that you can write the words correctly. If you don't, your answer will be wrong. You will hear the spelling once only.

Teacher's Book

The Teacher's Book has been designed to help you teach the material effectively and to allow you to see how the language and skills development relate directly to the IELTS test. You will also find the following:

- Extension exercises – exercises that help you give your students more practice with key skills.
- Alternative exercises – ideas that you can use to make the exercises more relevant for your students.
- Definitions – to help you with some of the key terms that are used in IELTS.

How to use the online modules

As well as the students book there are several online modules that each provide **6-8 hours** of further study. These can be used for homework or to reinforce what has been studied in the classroom. The core modules are:

- **Reading**
- **Listening**
- **Writing**
- **Speaking**
- **Grammar and Vocabulary**

In the Reading and Listening modules there is more practice with the same skills that students have studied but based on a different topic.

The Writing module builds on the skills that they have learnt in the unit and offers advice and model answers to help improve writing skills.

The Speaking module builds on knowledge of the topics that students have studied in the Student's book. This helps them to speak about the different topics with confidence and to develop the skills for the various parts of the Speaking Test. You can also see videos of students taking the test and complete exercises around this.

The Grammar and Vocabulary module reinforces and extends the vocabulary and grammar that has been studied in each unit of the book.

There are also a number of other online modules with specific learners in mind:

- **Chinese Pronunciation and Speaking**
- **Speaking Plus**

These modules look at the types of mistakes that students make at this level and from different language groups. The syllabus and exercises have been developed with insights from our corpus database of students speaking. Each module takes between 6 – 8 hours. Students can also analyse and view video content of Speaking Tests in these modules.

- **Arabic Spelling and Vocabulary**
- **Arabic Writing**
- **Chinese Spelling and Writing**
- **Writing Plus**

These modules use our database of past writing IELTS papers and Corpus research to look at the typical mistakes that students from the different language groups make on the Writing paper of the exam. They are encouraged to improve their writing skills and also avoid the common pitfalls that students make. Each of these modules provides **6-8 hours** of study.

- **Academic Study Skills**

The University Skills Module helps to bridge the gap between the skills that students learn studying IELTS and the ones that they need for the exam. The module shows students how they can use the knowledge they have and what they will need to work on when going to study in an English Language context for Higher Education.

About the IELTS Academic Module

Academic Reading

The Reading paper is made up of three different texts, which progress in level of difficulty. There is a total of 40 questions. Candidates have one hour to complete the information, this includes the time needed to transfer answers to the answer sheet. There is no extra time for this. Each question is worth one mark.

The texts are authentic and academic, but written for a non-specialist audience. Candidates must use information that appears in the text to answer the questions. They cannot use outside knowledge if they know about the topic. The types of texts are similar to the texts that you may find in a newspaper or magazine, so it is important for your students to get as much reading of these types of text as possible.

Texts sometimes contain illustrations. If a text contains technical terms a glossary will be provided.

The different task types are:

Multiple choice	Candidates will be asked to choose **one** answer from **four** options; choose **two** answers from **five** options or choose **three** answers from **seven** options.
Identifying information (True / False / Not Given)	Say if a statement given as a fact is True / False or Not Given.
Identifying the writer's views or claims (Yes / No / Not Given)	Say if a statement agrees with the opinions of the author or if it is not given in the text.
Matching information	Match information to paragraphs in a text.
Matching headings	Match a heading from a list to the correct part of the text.
Matching features	Match a list of statements to a list of possible answers (e.g. specific people or dates).
Matching sentence endings	Complete a sentence with a word or words from the text inside the word limit which is given.
Sentence completion	Complete a sentence with a word or words from the text inside the word limit which is given.
Notes/Summary/Table/Flow- chart completion	Complete with a suitable word or words from the text.
Labelling a diagram	Label a diagram with the correct word or word from a text. The words will be given in a box of possible answers.
Short-answer questions	Answer questions using words from the text inside the word limit

Academic Writing

There are two separate writing tasks. Candidates must answer both tasks.

Task 1

- Candidates should spend 20 minutes on this task.
- Candidates should write a minimum of 150 words. They will be penalised if they write less.
- Candidates need to describe and summarise a piece of visual information. The information may be presented in a diagram, map, graph or table.

Task 2

- Candidates should spend 40 minutes on this task.
- Candidates should write a minimum of 250 words. They will be penalised if they write less.
- Candidates need to write a discursive essay. They will be given an opinion, problem or issue that they need to respond to. They may be asked to provide a solution, evaluate a problem, compare and contrast different ideas or challenge an idea.

Listening

The Listening Paper is made up of four different texts. There are a total of 40 questions and there are 10 questions in each section. The paper lasts for approximately 30 minutes and students are given an extra 10 minutes to transfer their answers to the answer sheet. Each question is worth one mark.

In **Part 1** Candidates will hear a conversation between two people about a general topic with a transactional outcome (e.g. someone booking a holiday, finding out information about travel, returning a bought object to a shop).

In **Part 2** Candidates will hear a monologue or prompted monologue on a general topic with a transactional purpose (e.g. giving information about an event)

In **Part 3** Candidates will hear a conversation between two or three people in an academic setting (e.g. a student and a tutor discussing a study project)

In **Part 4** Candidates will hear a monologue in an academic setting (e.g. a lecture)

There may be one to three different task types in each section of the paper the task types are

Notes/Summary/Table/Flow-chart completion	Complete with a suitable word or words from the recording.
Multiple choice	Candidates will be asked to choose **one** answer from **three** alternatives or **two** answers from **five** alternatives.
Short-answer questions	Answer questions using words from the recording inside the word limit
Labelling a diagram, plan or map	Label a diagram/plan or map with a suitable word or words by choosing from a box with possible answers
Classification	Classify the given information in the question according to three different criteria (e.g. dates, names, etc.)
Matching	Match a list of statements to a list of possible answers in a box (e.g. people or dates)
Sentence completions	Complete a sentence with a word or words from the word limit which is given.

Speaking

The test is with an examiner and is recorded. The interview is made up of three parts.

Part 1

- Lasts for 4–5 minutes
- Candidates are asked questions on familiar topics like their hobbies, likes and dislikes.

Part 2

- Lasts for 3–4 minutes
- Candidates are given a task card with a topic (e.g. describe a special meal you have had) and are given suggestions to help them structure their talk. They have one minute to prepare their talk and then need to speak between 1 and 2 minutes on the topic.

Part 3

- Lasts for 4–5 minutes
- The examiner will ask candidates more detailed and more abstract questions about the topic in Part 2 (e.g. How are eating habits in your country now different from eating habits in the past)

In the Speaking test candidates are marked on Fluency and Coherence; Lexical Resource; Grammatical Range; Pronunciation.

What your students will need to do to get the band they require

Academic Reading

Candidates need to score approximately between 15 and 22 to obtain a Band 5 or 5.5 on Academic Reading.

Listening

Candidates need to score approximately between 16 and 22 to obtain a Band 5 or Band 5.5 on Listening.

Academic Writing and Speaking

The Public version of the IELTS Band Descriptors are available on www.ielts.org. To obtain a Band 5 students will need to illustrate all of the features of Band 5 and to obtain a Band 5.5 they will have to demonstrate all of the features of Band 5.5 and some of the features of Band 6.

How to connect knowledge of English language with the exam

Students beginning this course will already have a good knowledge of basic English. It is important to let them know that all their existing knowledge will be useful for the IELTS exam and will form the basis of developing further language knowledge and skills. The grammar, vocabulary and pronunciation they have already learned can be linked to different parts of the exam. In this book we help the student to do this.

Vocabulary

Vocabulary is obviously assessed in all four papers. Section 1 of the Listening Test and Part 1 of the speaking test, in particular, give students the chance to use the basic vocabulary they already know. In Listening they will hear words spelt out, numbers, dates, times etc. In speaking they will speak about familiar topics, such as their home town, family, hobbies and studies.

Students are encouraged to build on their existing vocabulary by learning and recording lexical sets around topics that commonly appear in the exam, including those in this book. Students should also focus on learning synonyms of the words they already know. This is because the speaking and writing papers test the range of vocabulary they use, and listening and reading papers rely heavily on students knowing different words for the same thing. Students should also focus on learning how the words they already know are used with other words. They should learn word partnerships, collocations and phrases rather than just individual, unrelated words.

Grammar

Students at this level are probably familiar with a few tenses, including the Present Simple and Past Simple. These are particularly useful in IELTS as students will need to use them in both writing tasks and the speaking test. This book will build on students' existing knowledge of tenses and show how they are used in different tasks. Different writing task 1 question types are associated with a range of grammar points. For example, when describing a process, students will need to use the Present Simple Passive; chart-based tasks either require comparatives and superlatives or the language of change, including verb/adverb and adjective/noun combinations. In the Speaking test, students will need past, present and future tenses. In Part 3 many questions are of the type 'What do you think will happen…?'

Connectives

Basic connectives that students already know (and, but, because, so, then) will be used in different writing tasks. Students will build on this knowledge and relate the connectives they learn to the task type. Process-type task 1 essays require candidates to use sequencing linkers (first, next, then, etc.), while comparison of data-type tasks will need connectives like whereas, while and compared with. In task 2 students will use a wide range of linkers to introduce similar and different ideas, examples and learn how to summarize and conclude.

Pronunciation

Your most important goal as an IELTS teacher is to ensure that students' speech is comprehensible. The speaking test assesses students on all aspects of pronunciation: sounds, word stress, sentence stress, connected speech and intonation. This is a quarter of the marks for speaking. The speaking sections of this book cover different aspects of pronunciation; however, you should listen closely to your students and identify where their pronunciation needs to be improved.

How to prepare your own materials for IELTS

Although there are many IELTS practice materials available, both in bookshops and online, you will probably find some of them too challenging for students at this level. You may therefore wish to create your own.

Reading

Written texts from regular textbooks at this level – or texts you've written yourself- can be useful IELTS preparation. Start by getting students to read the text quickly with a time limit of a minute or two. Ask them to cover the text and tell you what it is about- or write one sentence about the text. Then use some or all of the following ideas:

- Give each group or pair of students one paragraph. They find a suitable heading, write a one-sentence summary or highlight the topic sentence in one colour and supporting ideas in another colour.
- Students highlight all examples of cohesion in the text, including phrases like 'on the other hand', pronouns like 'they', 'it' and 'one' and synonyms/antonyms.
- Call out words or phrases from the text. Students 'race' to find them.
- Students find synonyms for some of the key words in the text.
- Students work out the meanings of unknown words from context.
- Students write their own short answer, True/False/Not Given and multiple choice questions in pairs and pass them to another group to answer.
- Students orally summarise the text in their own words.

Listening

For Listening as well you can use material from regular text books or from websites which have material for students of this level. Get students to do any of the following:

- Note down names, addresses, phone numbers, prices, etc.
- Listen and take notes. Write a summary from the notes.
- Give each group or pair a section of the tape-script. They make questions for another group to answer.

Students can also make their own listening materials. Give them a situation e.g. making a doctor's appointment. They work in pairs to write a dialogue. Correct their errors and then get them to act out the situation and record it on their phone or computer. They can design a form for another group to complete information such as day and time of appointment.

Writing

Writing task 1 materials can be easily created from any simple charts, pie charts and graphs you find in newspapers or online. Students can also generate their own data through a class survey, such as asking all members of the class their favourite food, hobbies or colours, or their month of birth. For homework, ask students to enter the data into Microsoft Excel or similar and create various types of charts, which they can use for writing practice.

For task 2, try the following ways of creating materials:

- Find- or write- model essays. Change the order of sentences and get students to put them into a logical order.
- Take some key words or phrases out of model essays and get students to replace them- give the missing words in a separate list for lower levels.
- Remove the introductions and conclusions from model essays and get students to reconstruct them.
- Use students' own essays –give them to another group and ask them to rewrite the essay with the opposing view.

Speaking

Turn every event into a speaking task. At the start of their first lesson of the week ask students to speak for 1-2 minutes about what they did at the weekend. After a holiday, festival or other local or national event, get them to talk about it. Ask them what they watched on TV the previous day, what happened in local or global news, a conversation they have had in the last week or a phone app they have downloaded. Anything can be turned into an IELTS speaking task!

Get students to listen to each other's talks and ask questions. When students show particular interest, let the conversation develop naturally as it would in Part 3 of the Speaking test.

How to deal with students' expectations at this level

The Level 1 course has been created in response to students' wish to learn about the IELTS test at the same time as developing their general English. The course reflects the needs of learners who are currently around IELTS 4-4.5. By the end of the course, the expectation is that they will have improved their score to between 5 and 5.5. Students need to be aware that improving their IELTS score is, realistically, a slow process. Any student preparing for the IELTS exam will be developing their general English at the same time. It is a process of getting used to the type of tasks which they will face in the exam while at the same time learning grammar, vocabulary and improving their abilities in the four skills. Mindset for IELTS 1 is the first in a series of 3 books, and students should expect to follow at least 2 of the courses to reach the absolute minimum requirement for study abroad. The third book in the series should take them up to band 7 to 7.5, which is the level where they can gain admission to most universities at undergraduate or postgraduate level.

Students should be made aware that simply attending class is not a guarantee of achieving the scores indicated on the books. They need to commit to a programme of self-study: learn new vocabulary, read and listen in English as much as possible and take every opportunity to speak in English, even if it is just with other learners like themselves.

How to use the material in a mixed-level class

There are two main ways to address the needs of a mixed-level class: the first involves adapting materials and activities so that they can be more or less challenging and assigning them to different groups of students; the second involves treating the higher level students as a resource to help the lower level students, while ensuring that the tasks given are useful for the higher-level learners too.

The Teachers book contains suggestions for alternative and extension activities. Many of these address the need for activities at different levels for students in a mixed-level class. For alternative activities, group all the higher-level students together and give instructions to them. Give instructions to the lower-level students for the basic activity. For extension activities which you feel are only suitable for some of the students, ensure the lower-level students also have a useful task. For them, activities which give them extra practice of the same language or skills are ideal. Try some of the following:

- If the unit has covered a tense, such as the simple present, ask them to write 5 more sentences in that tense.
- Ask them to re-read the text or audio-script again and use the dictionary to look up any unknown words which have not already been dealt with in the exercises.
- Get students to practise testing each other on the new words from the previous unit
- Get students re-do the speaking task from the previous unit with a different partner
- Ask them to listen again to recordings of themselves doing the previous task- identify errors or ways to improve.
- In groups or pairs get students to make a display chart for the wall on grammar or vocabulary covered so far in the course.

It is important that you don't always separate students in the class by level. For the main activities, it is generally useful for the more advanced students to be grouped with the lower-level ones. The lower-level ones will benefit from exposure to the more advanced language and skills of their classmates. The higher-level students benefit from having to explain language and concepts to other students. This is a linguistically challenging activity for them.

When working positively with mixed-level classes, you should be sensitive to the feelings of the students. Don't refer to the students as the 'less able' or 'lower-level' students. Just say 'Okay, for this activity, Danny, Chen, Mayuri and Qing will be working together'. If different groups are doing different activities, you don't need to stress this. Just give the instructions to different groups, rather than announcing to the whole class that different groups are doing different activities. If questioned, explain that 'these students will benefit from this activity' or 'This group needs more practice in this area'.

Always use the time when students are doing activities to monitor all the students so that you, as a teacher, are well aware of the different capabilities of different students. By knowing your class well and giving careful thought to their needs, you can ensure that a mixed-level class is successful.

READING

OUTCOMES

- answer questions using up to three words
- identify key words in a question
- scan a text to find specific information.

OUTCOMES

Ask students to focus on the outcomes of the lesson. Outcome 1 refers to the short answers task in the Reading paper. In IELTS, some question types require candidates to answer using a given number of words. Check that students understand 'up to 3 words'.

Outcomes 2 and 3 focus on skills that are generally useful in IELTS Reading. Check students understand the meaning of 'Key words'. Write a sentence on the board, e.g.

Jenny is from Beijing, which is the capital of China.

Ask a student to come to the board and underline the key words. Do another example, if needed.

Explain that it is important to be able to locate information very quickly as the biggest problem students have with the IELTS Reading paper is timing. This is what is meant, by 'scanning' a text.

Tell the students that the theme of the unit is relationships and elicit meaning (how we get along with other people, especially family and friends). Your 'relations' are your family members.

LEAD-IN

01 Write the example sentence on the board. Draw students' attention to the apostrophe 's'. Ask why it is after the 's' (you have 2 parents). Ask students 'Who is your aunt?' Elicit answer.

Put students into pairs to do the exercise. Monitor and ensure students are pronouncing the words correctly. Make sure the 's' sound can be heard, e.g. my uncle's son.

My aunt is my mother or father's sister.

My brother is my parents' son.

My cousin is my aunt or uncle's son or daughter.

My father-in-law is my husband or wife's father.

My grandfather is my mother or father's father.

My grandmother is my mother or father's mother.

My great-aunt is my grandmother or grandfather's sister.

My nephew is my brother or sister's son.

My niece is my brother or sister's daughter.

My uncle is my mother or father's brother.

Tell students who you live with (e.g.I live with my parents and my sister) and who you are also close to in your family (I am close to my mother). Explain that this means you speak to them or visit them often. Alternatively, use a student as an example (James lives with his mother and father. He is also close to his cousins). In the same pairs, students talk about their families.

02 Check the meaning of 'extended family'. Ask students if they live in an extended family. Tell them there are lots of advantages of this type of family. Can students think of any?

Ask students to look at the 5 advantages listed. Students tell their partners one or two that they feel are important.

Ask students to read the text ONLY for the purpose of checking if any of the advantages are listed. Tell them that it is important in IELTS to read with a purpose.

Alternative

Give one of the advantages to each pair. They skim read the text and decide together if their advantages are mentioned.

2, 3, 4 and 5 are mentioned in the text.

03 Draw students' attention to the tip. Explain that they will not know every word in the Reading paper and it is important to avoid worrying about unknown words. It is often possible to work out the meaning by reading the other words around it. Tell students they will do an exercise to practise this.

Tell students that starting with the words they know or 'easy answers' is a good technique in the Reading paper. Ask them to read through the list of words in the left hand column and identify the ones they already know. They should try to find the meanings of these words from the right hand column.

Do an example. Ask them to find the word 'value'. Read about the sentence with 'value' in it. Ask which word or phrase from the list could replace it (believe something is important) and then go to the text to read the context of any unknown words and complete the exercise.

1 h   2 g   3 a   4 b   5 f   6 c   7 e   8 d

04 This is a fun activity in which students experience scanning the text under pressure. Get students to put into words (in L1 if necessary) HOW you locate information quickly.

grandparents' stories (D)   cousin's wedding (A)   young adults (E)   extended families (B)   come and go (G)   Italian proverb (F)

To find information quickly, don't read every word. Don't try to say the words. Move your eyes quickly across and down the text. Use your finger if you find it useful.

05 Remind students of the meaning of 'key words'. Check students have identified the correct words.

> 1 percentage / children / extended families / Asia, the Middle East, South America, Sub-Saharan Africa
> 2 grandparents / less busy / stressed / parents
> 3 young adults / think / living alone

06 Read through the advice box with students before they answer the questions in exercise 05.

> 1 over 40%   2 They are often retired.
> 3 (They think it will be) exciting.

07 Tell students that this activity focuses on common errors that students make in the exam. These include not following instructions by exceeding the number of words specified, using words not in the text or careless errors such as spelling.

> 1 b   2 d   3 a   4 c

08 Focus students' attention on the tip. Explain that words that are not 'key' words are often 'grammar' words. Elicit some grammar words. Explain that these can be left out in order to meet the word limit.

> 1 over 40%   2 grandparents' stories
> 3 lonely   4 your grandmother

GRAMMAR

The aim of exercises 09, 10 and 11 is to get students to notice the use of the Simple Present tense and frequency adverbs in the text. Give them time to study the text and come up with rules by themselves. Being aware of which tense(s) is/are being used in a text can help students to understand the meaning and answer questions correctly.

09
> 1 present simple   2 b

10
> 1 always   2 often   3 often ; (not) always
> 4 usually   5 Sometimes

11
> The frequency adverb is usually between the subject and the verb. (*I often cook*). When the verb is 'to be', the adverb comes after the verb. (*It is always cold.*) Some frequency adverbs can also start a sentence. (*Sometimes I watch TV.*)

Extension

Get students to talk about their own habits using the Simple Present tense and adverbs of frequency.

12 Remind students of the key points of the lesson:
- Read the instructions carefully.
- Highlight key words in the question.
- Use scanning skills to locate information.
- Use context to help with meaning of unknown words (only if needed to answer the question)

Give students a maximum of 15 minutes to do the Practice exercise under exam conditions.

> 1 social media   2 geographically mobile
> 3 less security   4 convenience
> 5 mental health problems

WRITING

> ## OUTCOMES
>
> - describe a process (Writing Part 1)
> - use sequencing expressions to describe the order of stages in a process
> - use the present simple passive to describe a process
> - write an introduction and overview.

OUTCOMES

This lesson relates to writing task 1. The first 3 outcomes relate specifically to describing a process. The fourth outcome, write an introduction and overview, relates to all task 1 types. Tell students that when we describe a process we are interested in what happens rather than in who does the various actions involved. Therefore we use the Passive voice, e.g. 'Water is heated'.

An introduction – or introductory sentence-in task 1 is often a paraphrase of the question- it tells the reader what kind of data this is.

An overview presents the data in summary form.

Examples

Introductory sentence

The diagram shows the process of producing tea from planting to its arrival in the shops.

Overview

The process consists of eight main stages- from planting and plucking on the plantation, drying, withering, sorting and packaging in the factory to, distribution and sales all over the world.

Both of these need to be present. An introduction is always at the beginning. The overview can be anywhere in the text but is most likely to be after the introduction or at the end.

LEAD-IN

01 Give some examples of 'celebrations', such as birthdays or festivals. Students add more examples. Tell students typical foods you eat on special occasions. Students talk in pairs. Help them with names of equipment or vocabulary to describe the processes involved in preparing the food.

02 Ask students if they know where Sri Lanka is (an island to the south of India). They are going to read descriptions of equipment needed to make a Sri Lankan dish called 'stringhoppers'. The aim of this activity is to expose students to the language they might need for describing objects. Check answers.

> 1 B   2 A   3 C

03 In this part of the activity, students focus on the language which enabled them to do the above exercise.

> **Materials:** plastic, metal, wood, cloth
> **Parts:** handles, base, tray
> **Shapes:** round, square, triangle, rectangle

Advice

Students could add some more materials, parts and shapes to the table.

04 The aim of this activity is to demonstrate that students do not need to be familiar with the process described or even know the key vocabulary used as a lot of information is provided in the task. While key vocabulary is given, this is usually in note form. Students will need to change the notes into full sentences, using appropriate structures.

1 c	2 b	3 f	4 a	5 d	6 e

Grammar focus: the present simple passive

05 Write the sentences 'We make them with rice' and 'They are made with rice' on the board.

Ask a student to come to the board and highlight the subjects and verbs of the sentences in different colours.

Active verb in present simple	Verb 'to be in present simple	Past participle

We make them with rice.   They are made with rice.

Ask who 'We' are (people who make stringhoppers).

Ask who 'They' are (stringhoppers)

'Make' is active because the subject (we) does the action.

'Are made' is passive because the subject (they) has the action done to them.

Label the verb forms as above. Point out that 'to be' (in any tense) plus past participle are needed to form the passive.

Students complete the exercise.

1 are picked	2 are used	3 is needed	4 grown

Sequencing words

06 Linking your ideas together appropriately is very important in IELTS writing. Each task type requires different types of linkers. For describing a process, students need to make it clear in which order the steps take place. The words in the box are all suitable for this kind of task. As students do exercise 6, they need to think about the logical order of the steps as well as the grammar.

1 First	2 After	3 Then / Next
4 The next stage	5 Next / Then	6 Finally

Alternative

If your class is doing well with this lesson, refer them back to the pictures and elicit the steps before doing this exercise. This will give them a chance to practise the vocabulary and the use of the Passive as practised in previous exercises.

Introduction and overview

07 Stress that the introduction and overview are not the same and both are essential to any task 1 essay, not just describing a process. The difference between the two is that the introduction tells the reader what type of data it is (e.g. whether it is diagrams showing a process or charts with data on exports from two different countries). The overview tells the reader something about the data itself without going into detail.

a overview	b introduction

08

a and d are not overviews

Explain that:

a. is an introduction

d is an introduction plus first stage. There does not appear to be an overview, but the overview doesn't have to be after the introduction; it could also be at the end.

Model answer

09 The model answers presented in this book are designed to be achievable for the students at this level. They are simple but correct rather than band 8/9 answers.

> 1 The diagram demonstrates the process of preparing stringhoppers, a kind of noodle dish.
> 2 There are six main stages in the process, beginning with grinding the rice and making a dough and ending with using a steamer to cook the stringhoppers.
> 3 First, Next, After that, then, The final stage is
> 4 is put, is mixed, (is) formed, is put, is pushed, are placed, are ... cooked
> 5 a metal piece of equipment with two handles and holes in it; round baskets made of thin pieces of wood
> 6 grind, rice, dough, steamer, grinder, flour, stringhopper press, stringhopper mats, cook, serve, spicy, curries

10 Before students attempt exercise 10, ask them to look at the pictures and say some words that they could use in the task. Give them a few examples, such as 'wash' or 'cook'.

The exercise involves finding the past participle of the verbs in the box. 3 of the verbs are irregular (put-put, shake-shook and take-taken). For weaker classes, you could elicit/teach past participle forms of the verbs in advance.

1 spread; shaken	2 collected; transported / taken	
3 removed	4 washed	5 taken out
6 cooked; added	7 checked	8 put
9 stuck		

EXAM SKILLS

11 Depending on your class, you could get them to do the practice essay with or without reference to the lesson.

The pictures show the stages in the production of cherry jam. There are a number of processes involved, from picking the fruit from the tree to putting it into jars ready to sell.

First, a sheet is spread on the ground under the tree and the tree is shaken by a mechanical arm to get the cherries down from the tree. Then, the cherries are collected and transported by lorry to the processing plant. There the leaves and the stems are removed and then the stone is taken out with a metal spike. Next, sugar, lemon juice and pectin are added to the cherries and the jam is cooked. After that, the quality of the jam is checked and then the jam is put into jars. A lid is put on top of the jars to keep the jam fresh. Finally, a label is added and the jam is ready to be sold in the shops.

Feedback

When marking essays, do so positively. Tick the introduction and overview as well as examples of sequencing linkers and passive forms. Use a different colour to underline errors. Use a correction code to encourage students to correct their own errors rather than making the correction for them, e.g.:

Sp-spelling

Gr- grammar

T-tense

P-punctuation

L-linking

Provide a positive comment at the end as well as a suggestion for how the student can improve, e.g.

'Good use of linkers but check your passive forms'.

LISTENING

OUTCOMES

- identify the speakers in a conversation
- listen for numbers
- answer multiple-choice questions.

OUTCOMES

Draw students' attention to the outcomes. Point out that in parts 1 and 3 of the listening test there are two speakers (sometimes 3 in part three).Reassure students that the voices will sound very different (often male and female). Listening for numbers can be challenging as numbers like '15/50' sound similar. There are several types of question in the Listening test. In this unit multiple choice (choosing an answer from several options) will be practised.

01 The aim here is to check that students understand what is meant by 'everyday situations'.

> C, D

02 Play the recording once. Students only need to identify the situation after the first listening.

Transcript 02

Conversation 1

Manager:	Good evening, Willowtree Hotel. How can I help?
Customer:	Hello, I'd like to make a reservation in your restaurant for next Saturday evening.
Manager:	Next Saturday? If you hold on, I'll just check … So … for how many people?
Customer:	I need a table for twelve – it's my husband's 30th birthday, so we're having a celebration dinner.

Conversation 2

Sales assistant:	Good afternoon, can I help you?
Customer:	Yes, I'm looking for a gift for my sister. She's going to be 18 next week. So I thought a piece of jewellery would be nice.
Sales assistant:	Good idea! Do you have anything particular in mind – a necklace perhaps?
Customer:	Mm, she has so many necklaces. I was thinking of a pair of earrings, possibly.
Sales assistant:	Does she have a favourite colour?
Customer:	Mm, she likes blue ….

Conversation 1: D	Conversation 2: C

03 Play the recording a second time. This time students identify the gender (Male or Female) of the speakers.

1 M	2 F	3 F	4 M

04 After listening again, students choose the correct option. Point out that the 'wrong' answer will usually be mentioned in the listening in some way to distract them.

5 A	6 B

05 This exercise give students practice in identifying the difference between similar-sounding numbers.

Transcript 03

a the 3rd	b $10.50	c the 6th	d 70
e 19	f 62	g £110	h the 27th

a 3rd	b $10.50	c 6th	d 70
e 19	f 62	g £110	h 27th

LEAD-IN

Additional activity

Students work in pairs. They take it in turns to say one of the numbers in each pair. The other student says 'one' or 'two' or points at the number he/she has heard. If the correct number can't be identified, you can intervene and check the student has pronounced the number correctly.

06-10 Students are introduced to ways of finding the correct answer even though all the options are mentioned in the text. Often speakers say one of the options and then correct themselves. This is a technique students should look out for. These exercises help students with a detailed listening which allows them to identify why the other answers are incorrect.

Transcript 04

Customer:	I need a table for twelve – it's my husband's 30th birthday, so we're having a celebration dinner.
Manager:	So that's twelve people for the sixteenth.
Customer:	No, no, it's the day after – the seventeenth – Saturday the seventeenth, at eight o'clock.
Manager:	Ah, yes, of course. A party of twelve for the Saturday? Oh, I'm sorry, but I'm afraid our main restaurant is fully booked that evening but we do have a small room available for private hire. It can seat up to 20 people, so there would be plenty of space for 12 of you.
Customer:	That sounds perfect.

06

1 B	2 C

07

1 17th	2 20

08 Transcript 05

Customer:	That sounds perfect.
Manager:	Excellent. Now we offer a set three-course menu for £23 per person and we can also supply you with a birthday cake at no extra charge. How does that sound?
Customer:	That sounds good. So how much would that cost in total?
Manager:	Let me see – for the food and the room, that will come to £318.
Customer:	Did you say three hundred and eighty pounds?
Manager:	No, three hundred and eighteen.
Customer:	OK, I think I'd like to go ahead and make a booking.
Manager:	OK, I'll just take your details.

B

09 Transcript 06

Sales assistant:	Good afternoon, can I help you?
Customer:	Yes, I'm looking for a gift for my sister. She's going to be 18 next week. So I thought a piece of jewellery would be nice.
Sales assistant:	Good idea! Do you have anything particular in mind – a necklace perhaps?
Customer:	Mm, she has so many necklaces. I was thinking of a pair of earrings, possibly.
Sales assistant:	Does she have a favourite colour?
Customer:	Mm, she likes blue …
Sales assistant:	What about this pair? They have some beautiful little blue stones.
Customer:	Mm … They're quite nice, I suppose.
Sales assistant:	They're silver, and they're handmade, so you won't find anything like them anywhere else.
Customer:	Oh, really? So, how much are they?
Sales assistant:	Well they *were* thirty pounds, but actually we've got a sale on at the moment, so they're a little cheaper – only twenty pounds. So you can save ten pounds!
Customer:	Great. I'll take them.
Sales assistant:	And would you like me to giftwrap them for you?
Customer:	How much do you charge for that?
Sales assistant:	For £4 we give you a pretty box and your own choice of wrapping paper. Or for £5 you can have our luxury wrapping service, which includes a silver box and silver ribbon. And if you would like a card to write your own personal message, that will be £2 extra.
Customer:	Well, it's a special birthday so I'll take the luxury option. But I already have a card, thank you.
Sales assistant:	That's fine. I'll do that for you now. And how would you like to pay – cash or card?

1 B	2 B

10 Transcript 07

Customer:	Oh, really? So, how much are they?
Sales assistant:	Well they *were* thirty pounds, but actually we've got a sale on at the moment, so they're a little cheaper – only twenty pounds. So you can save ten pounds!

1 30/thirty	2 20/twenty	3 10/ten

Option

In exercise 10 you might want to point out the stress on 'were' This word would not normally be stressed so it is a clue that the earrings are no longer £30.

Multiple choice questions

> **Paraphrase**
>
> Saying or writing a phrase, sentence or text in different words while still giving the same message. To paraphrase well, structures should be changed as well as words and phrases.

11 The skill of paraphrase is very important in all parts of the IELTS exam. For example, in writing you can avoid repetition, in speaking you can demonstrate a wider range of vocabulary and in listening and reading it will help you identify the answers. Exercise 11 is an introduction to this crucial skill. Exercise 12 provides further practice while introducing them to the exam skills activity.

1 c	2 e	3 d	4 a	5 b	

12
1 The relationship between the people
2 The type of event
3 Colour
4 The meaning of something
5 Food
6 Presents

Extension

Depending on the level of your class you can incorporate the use of synonyms and paraphrase into all classroom activities. For example, get them to say 'Hello' and 'Goodbye' in different ways at the beginning and end of lessons.

EXAM SKILLS

Students have the opportunity to practise the skills learnt in the unit.

Transcript 08

Mark: Hi there, Nam! You aren't *still* working on your history assignment, are you?

Nam: Hi, Victor! No, I'm taking a break. I'm looking at some photos, actually – a family celebration. Do you want to see them?

Mark: So, who's the cute baby in this picture here?

Nam: She's my niece – my brother's daughter. Her name's Tae-Hee. She's one year old in this picture. It's a very important birthday in Korea – we call it 'Dol' or Doljanchi. It's a very special celebration – in fact, I think it's probably more important than a wedding or a graduation! And we invite all our family and friends and sometimes our neighbours. Here's a picture of the restaurant where we celebrated Tae-Hee's big day.

Mark: What a lovely place – and a beautiful garden, too.

Nam: Yes, it's a perfect location for taking photographs. Can you see me just there next to the trees?

Mark: Ah yes, I like your hat! And I like the red and silver hat Tae-Hee's wearing too. It's really pretty.

Nam: Yes, it's a traditional hat for a girl. Baby boys wear a different one – all black. It looks very serious!

Mark: That's a bit boring. Black and silver would be more interesting. What's Tae-Hee wearing round her skirt?

Nam: That's a little purse. Boy babies wear this too. It's made of silk and it means good luck in our culture. And she's wearing a belt too. Look – do you see? The belt means she will have a long life!

Mark: And what's this on the table there? It's very colourful.

Nam: It's rice cakes.

Mark: I've never seen anything like that before. It looks like a rainbow!

Nam: We always eat rice cakes at a baby's party. There are usually 12 different types of them on the table. Look – this rice cake is completely orange in colour and this one here is bright green!

Mark: It looks like a vegetable!

Nam: Now, look – this is me with my brother's wife, Mi-Cha. We get on really well together.

Mark: What are you holding?

Nam: Oh, it's a little bag. All the guests get a gift bag at the end of the party. And inside there's a present from the baby's parents. It's really fun to open it because you don't know what you'll get. So it could be a candle, or some chocolates. Guess what I got? You can see it in this next photo.

Mark: It looks like a box of tea. But shouldn't it be the other way round – the baby gets the presents?

Nam: Well, the baby receives money from the guests, so in a way you're right! And actually, I've got my present right here. So, why don't we open the box right now and have a cup of tea? Then we can try to finish our assignments.

Mark: Sounds good to me!

1 A	2 A	3 C	4 B	5 C	6 B

Extension

If students have found this difficult, you could play the recording again, stopping after the answer to each question has been given. Get students to identify the clues which should help them find the answer, e.g. 'sister' in question 1.

SPEAKING

OUTCOMES

- use simple adjective-noun collocations relating to family
- answer simple questions about your family
- give full answers to Part 1 questions.

OUTCOMES

Students will learn how to extend their answers without talking too much. Part 1 is a series of questions on familiar topics and the easiest part of the speaking test.

LEAD-IN

01 This activity will give you an opportunity to assess students' speaking ability at the start of the lesson. Demonstrate by talking about one of your family members (real or made up) for about 20 seconds. Don't spend a lot of time correcting errors at this stage as you can do so in the final practice activity. The aim of this is just to get students talking and help them understand what 20 seconds feels like.

The word 'collocation' is introduced here. This is a word students should become familiar with as you can use it when teaching them about any part of the exam, and when correcting their speaking and writing. It is important for students to understand that words should not be learnt in isolation but in 'chunks' or phrases.

Collocation

Words used together more frequently than would occur by chance, for example 'heavy rain', 'strong wind'.

Chunks

Chunks include collocations but also groups of words that occur together frequently for grammatical reasons, such as 'I'm going home' or 'I've never been there'.

Exercises 02 and 03 practise collocations with 'family'.

02

> (not) a large family, a small family, a typical family, a close, happy family

Transcript 09

Examiner: Let's talk about family. So, tell me about your family.

Hoi Chin: My family? Well, my family isn't a large family. It's quite a small family, in fact – and quite a typical family for my country. Just my parents, my older brother and me. So, I'm the baby of the family! I think we're a close, happy family. We do a lot of things together, particularly preparing food – and eating it of course!

03

> You can't say 'a best family'

GRAMMAR: ADVERBS OF FREQUENCY

04 After students answer the questions, draw their attention to the frequency adverbs (sometimes, often, usually and never). Give a few examples about your own activities (e.g. I often go out for dinner, I rarely cook), and ask students to speak about the activities in exercise 05. Monitor and correct errors you hear.

Transcript 10

Examiner: How often do you go out with your family?

Boy: Sorry? Can you repeat that?

Examiner: How often do you go out with your family?

Boy: Well … we're a close family, we like spending a lot of time together. We try to go out once a week – usually at weekends – on Saturdays or Sundays. We all really like being in the fresh air so we often go for a long walk along the beach. We enjoy going early in the morning when it's quiet. We never go when it's crowded! We live near a big park, so we sometimes go there. We usually go for a long

walk and sometimes have a barbeque by the lake. Sometimes our cousin comes along too. He loves running around in the sunshine. He even enjoys swimming in the lake, so it's a good day out for him too!

> 1 once a week.
> 2 on Saturdays or Sundays / at weekends
> 3 to the beach.
> 4 They usually go for a long walk.
> 5 His cousin sometimes comes with them.

Extension

Students can talk about other activities they do with members of their family. Help them with vocabulary. They can practise other expressions, such as 'once a week', 'three times a year'.

06 This exercise helps students to understand some common questions that the examiner may ask about his or her family. It also provides more speaking practice. It is often a good idea for students to change their partner several times during a lesson to give them a chance to develop their confidence in speaking to different partners. Move around the classroom and listen closely, correcting errors you hear.

> 1 c   2 d   3 b   4 a

07 This exercise practises listening for specific information. After listening, ask students to talk about Hoi Chin's family. By now the information will be familiar to them, giving them the opportunity to focus on the language they are using and pronunciation. If necessary, give students some guidance in comparing Hoi Chin's family to theirs, e.g. Hoi Chin's family is small but mine in smaller. I am an only child!'

Transcript 11

Hoi Chin: My family? Well, my family isn't a large family. It's quite a small family in fact – and quite a typical family for my country. Just my parents, my older brother and me. So, I'm the baby of the family! I think we're a close, happy family. We do a lot of things together, particularly preparing food – and eating it of course! Yes, we spend a lot of time in the kitchen. My father's a very good cook – he's much better than my mother. My brother's getting married next year, so I'm really looking forward to having a sister-in-law! And who knows? Perhaps our family will get bigger in future! I'd love to have a niece or a little nephew to take to the park one day. Yes, I really want to be an aunt!

2 close	3 eating	
4 cook	5 married	6 /7 nephew/niece

Alternative

Stronger students/classes can close their books and talk about Hoi Chin's family from memory.

08 Ensure students understand the question, 'Who are you most similar to in your family?' If you wish you can give a 'model' answer about yourself to illustrate the meaning.

Transcript 12

Student A:	I get on really well with both of my sisters. The older one's at university in Australia, so I don't see her very often anymore. The younger one still lives at home though, and we spend all of our free time together.
Student B:	I'm a lot like my father. We look similar and have the same interests.
Student C:	Most people say that I'm similar to my father because we both have green eyes and black hair. However, I think that I'm more similar to my mother in character. We're both easy going and calm, so I think it's a mixture of both.

1 Student B	2 Student A	3 Student C

(student A answered a different question – 'who do you get on with best in your family?')

09 Go through the information in the box with the students. Point out that the highlighted words provide useful ways to give extra information about your answer.

> Sample answers, but many others are possible
> 1 ... because they are the most important people in my life.
> 2 ... but we still get along very well.
> 3 ... and she is going to move to a different city with her husband.
> 4 ... so I don't spend as much time with him as I want to.
> 5 ... even though he is quite a bit older.

Alternative

Students can give their answers orally instead of writing them down, or they can write them, then cover them and practise saying them to their partner.

PRONUNCIATION

10 Many students mispronounce words which add an extra syllable when they change form by adding an 's'. This is true of plural forms as well as third person 's'. Pay particular attention to students' pronunciation of 'watches' and 'chooses'.

Transcript 13

> asks, chooses, enjoys, keeps, plays, talks, wants, watches,

> /s/ asks, keeps, talks, wants
> /z/ enjoys, plays
> /iz/ chooses, watches

11 Check meaning of 'annoys' (does things that make you don't like or make you angry). This exercise focuses on the pronunciation of third person 's' so focus on monitoring that.

Transcript 14

Examiner:	Is there anyone in your family who annoys you sometimes?
A:	My father watches football on TV and shouts a lot.
B:	My brother plays on the computer all the time.
C:	My mother keeps telling me to tidy my room.

Extension

Depending on your class, you could also highlight sentence stress (the fact that words that carry the meaning are stressed rather than grammar words), e.g.

My <u>father</u> <u>watches</u> <u>football</u> on <u>TV</u> and <u>shouts</u> a lot.

12 Exercise 12 also focuses on pronunciation of third person 's' but also gives students practice of the grammar and vocabulary they have learnt in this lesson.

EXAM SKILLS

Pair students up with someone they have not yet worked with if possible. The role of the listening partner is important. They should practise 'active listening' by listening for language from the lesson or any new language their partner produces.

Feedback

It is important to students to receive feedback on their main speaking tasks throughout the course. It is also important to develop students' confidence when speaking. Therefore, don't over-correct. Decide what errors to focus on. For example, ones that interfere with communication, such as pronunciation of 'rake' and 'lake'

Circulate around listening to different students. Don't interrupt them but note down significant errors. These may be those connected to today's lesson or those made frequently or by many students, or those that affect communication.

After the students have finished the activity, write the errors on the board and ask students to correct them. They can come up to the board and use a different colour to make the correction. Always focus on what students have done well and praise them for taking an active part in the speaking task.

READING

> ### OUTCOMES
>
> - respond to sentence completion questions
> - skim read a text
> - recognise paraphrase
> - practise using the present simple and past simple.

OUTCOMES

Draw students' attention to the outcomes. This lesson introduces the key IELTS reading skill of skimming.

> **Skimming**
>
> To read a text quickly to get the main ideas. When you skim a text you do not have to read every word.

> **Scanning**
>
> Moving your eyes across a text to find specific information, ignoring everything that is not relevant.

Tell students that as soon as they see a text they should 'skim' it to get the general idea.

Paraphrase (see definition in Unit 1) is one of the most important skills in IELTS because it is needed in all four of the papers. Point out that in the reading paper, questions will often include a paraphrase of the actual words used in the text. Therefore, students need to get used to looking for similar words when looking for the answers.

In reading, recognising tenses can help students to understand the meaning.

LEAD-IN

01 Model the activity by describing your own house (real or imagined). Ask a few students sample questions based on the prompts, e.g. 'Doris, is your house big or small?'

Students then work in pairs to ask and answer questions about their own houses. Circulate, listen and correct errors in grammar and pronunciation.

02 Ask students to look at the pictures and captions. Choose a student to model an answer. Elicit 'I would like to live in a luxury apartment in the city because it has good views and is near the shops and restaurants' (or similar). Students exchange their ideas in pairs.

> **Alternative**
>
> Ask all the students who chose a house in the country to go to one corner of the room, those who chose a luxury apartment to another and those who chose a caravan a third. When they get there, they share their reasons with the others who made the same choice. They return to their group and share the reasons they heard from others.

03 Tell students that most people live in houses or flats but there are some other types of accommodation. Elicit some of them. Ask students where they usually stay when they go on holiday. Hotels, guest houses etc. are possible but tell them there are some unusual places you can stay on holiday too.

Ask students to match the pictures to the words in the box. Check answers. Give students the chance to give their opinions about them, saying which they would or would not like to live in.

Write the words SKIMMING and SCANNING on the board. Read through the box with the students. Tell them that both skills will be used in every IELTS reading text.

A tree house	B shipping container homes
C igloo	D houseboat

04 Tell students that speed is very important in IELTS reading. Therefore, in this exercise, they will have only one minute to read the passage. It is not possible to do a careful reading in that time, so they need to move their eyes quickly, ignoring 'grammar words' and noticing 'key' words. Give an example by asking them to glance quickly at paragraph A. Point out that 'keywords' here include 'houseboat' and 'Holland', as these carry information about the main ideas of the text.

> **Key words**
>
> Key words are the important words that carry the main meaning of the passage.

b

05 Ask students to find the key words in the box quickly.

> **Alternative**
>
> If students have a print copy, get them to highlight the words. Make it a race to see who can highlight all the words first.

06 Students should tell you the answer. Reiterate that BOTH reading skills are important. They complement each other as they are used for different purposes.

exercise 5 – scanning; exercise 4 – skimming

Exercises 07 and 08 both practise paraphrase. Exercise 7 contains words and short phrases, whereas exercise 8 practises identifying paraphrase of entire sentences. Emphasise that if students are not able to do this, they are likely to pick the wrong answer.

07

1 c	2 e	3 a	4 f	5 b	6 d

08

1 B	2 A	3 B

Get students to prepare their own exercise to practise paraphrase. Each student writes 3 -5 short phrases on a piece of paper. They pass it to their partner, who has to paraphrase it.

E.g. Student A: Have a great weekend! Student B: Enjoy yourself on Saturday and Sunday!

Advice

This kind of activity can be done regularly to reinforce the idea of paraphrase throughout the course.

09 Read through the 'how to' box with the students, relating it closely to the example.

Ask students to highlight the key words in the questions.

Elicit similar words for each key word.

Ask students to find the relevant sentence in the text.

Ask how many words they are looking for. Remind them the words must be from the text.

Example

1. The key words are 'two people', 'transparent house' and 'love.

   Example similar words are 'a couple', 'see-through house' and 'like'.

   Students need to read the last sentence of Paragraph B.

   'Suit everyone' fits grammatically after 'wouldn't' and the meaning contrasts with 'the two people…love it'.

   After writing their answers, get students to check with a partner. If they have different answers, they work together to decide which is correct.

1 suit everyone	2 draw attention
3 reindeer skins	4 busy lives

GRAMMAR FOCUS: PAST SIMPLE AND PRESENT SIMPLE

10-12 Tell students that the ability to identify tenses and the reason they have been used is important in the reading test. These exercises provide a brief awareness-raising and basic practice. The grammar will be revisited in other sections of the unit.

10
1 c	
2 a present simple	b present simple
c past simple	d past simple

11
1 live	2 have	3 moved	4 spends	5 preferred

12
1 shares	2 lived	3 stayed	4 has	5 moved

EXAM SKILLS

13 Do this as exam practice, but remind students to skim first, highlight key words in the questions, check the number of words required, take the words from the passage and check the grammar when they've finished.

1 roast chicken	2 homesick and sad
3 her parents	4 Ping and Pong
5 forest	6 feel at home / feel welcome

Alternative

If you prefer, you could guide the students through the practice activity step by step. This will depend on the level and confidence of your class.

Extension

The text could be further exploited in different ways, for example:

* Students compare the English and German homes and families (orally or in writing)
* Students write some more questions and pass them to a partner to answer.
* Students underline examples of regular and irregular past tense forms.
* Choose a few sentences for students to paraphrase.

WRITING

OUTCOMES

* describe changes over time as shown on a map
* use prepositions to explain location
* use past tense verbs forms (active and passive) to describe change.

OUTCOMES

This unit relates to the writing task 1 questions which ask candidates to describe a map. They usually have to describe how an area has changed over time. The lesson focuses on the language that will be useful for this task type such as prepositions of place like next to, in front of, behind and verbs that describe change, such as move and create. Point out that the lesson will include useful language to describe a university campus, which students will need in the future.

LEAD-IN

01 Students read the words in the box. Help them with any unknown words. There may be some discussion about what facilities a university campus usually has. In the UK all of them can be found on some campuses, but a bank or post office is not found on most of them. 'Halls of residence' is a UK term for what Americans call 'dormitories'.

Alternative

If you have a stronger class, elicit what facilities can be found on a campus without looking at the box.

All of the places listed may be on a campus.

02 Students have a quick look at the maps and see which of the facilities mentioned in exercise 1 are shown.

The following are shown on the campus maps: bus stop, recreation area, cafés, car park, library, laboratories, Students' Union, squash courts, gym, halls of residence, tennis courts, football pitch, table tennis tables

GRAMMAR FOCUS: PREPOSITIONS OF PLACE

03 There are two purposes to this activity. It exposes students to examples of the kind of sentences they will need to do the task, and it familiarises them with the maps.

Ask students to read the tip. Point out that although prepositions are short words, they can make a big difference to meaning.

> Sentences 1, 2, 5 and 7 are true.

Extension

Students could highlight the prepositions in the sentences.

04 Tell students they need to focus closely on the map to do this exercise.

1 next to	2 of	3 between
4 opposite	5 on	6 in
7 to/on	8 of	

05 This exercise should be done orally. Model the first one. Students work in pairs to complete the sentences so that they are true for the campus as it is today. Advise them to alternate with their partner.

> *Sample answers*
> 1 The halls of residence are on the left side of the campus.
> 2 The laboratories are opposite the Founder's Building.
> 3 The bus stop is in the top right-hand corner.
> 4 The recreation area is next to the laboratories (and the Scott Library).
> 5 The table tennis tables are in front of /next to the Scott Library.
> 6 The Students' Union is between the gym and the bus stop.

06 Give students a few minutes to read the model answer quietly to themselves.

07 This is a very important point. It is especially important that students understand the difference between the introductory sentence and the overview. Tell students that in task 1 an introductory and concluding sentence is enough due to the shorter length of the essay. If students have access to a print copy, get them to highlight these features in different colours.

Introductory sentence: The first sentence of the essay, in which the candidate describes the type of data.

Overview: A brief summary of the main trends revealed in the data. This can be anywhere in the essay, although after the introductory sentence or at the end would be the most logical.

Concluding sentence: The last sentence which is usually a summary of the main points made in the essay.

> 1 b Introductory sentence: *The two maps show changes to the campus of Sunnyhills University between 1995 and today.*
>
> 2 c Concluding sentence: *So, it is clear that the university changed and expanded during the period.*
>
> 3 a Overview: *We can see that the university made many changes to the campus during this period, including new buildings and recreation facilities.*

08-10 There will probably be some words in the essay that are new to students. Make sure they have time to note them down.

08
> 1 was relocated, increased, were moved, was built, were demolished, created, developed, changed, expanded
> 2 in front of, to the right, in the top left-hand corner, the far left of the campus, opposite

09
1 in addition, what is more	2 whereas, however
3 during this period, in the past	4 we can see, it is clear

10
1 relocated	2 created, developed
3 demolished	4 expanded, increased (in size)

Advice

Vocabulary exercises are an opportunity to instil good habits in students. They should have a separate notebook or section of their notebook for vocabulary.

When referring students to the tip, point out that they need to show that they know a range of vocabulary so they should not repeat words too often. In particular, they should learn different words for commonly used words like 'and' and 'but.

GRAMMAR FOCUS: PAST SIMPLE – REGULAR AND IRREGULAR FORMS

11-12

11
> *Made, was* and *built* are irregular.   The infinitives are:
> made – make   was – be   increased – increase
> moved – move   created – create
> developed – develop   built – build
> changed – change   expanded – expand

12
> | | | | |
> |---|---|---|---|
> | 1 cut | 2 became | 3 caught | 4 needed |
> | 5 put | 6 were | 7 dug | 8 planted |
>
> *Needed* and *planted* are regular.

Advice

When teaching grammar, be aware that students will take time, repeated exposure and plenty of practice to learn each grammar point. You should come back to points again whenever students encounter them in new contexts.

Extension

Check students are able to pronounce the past tense forms 'caught', 'needed' , 'planted', 'expanded' and 'created'

GRAMMAR FOCUS: PAST SIMPLE – ACTIVE AND PASSIVE

13 Put sentences 1 to 4 up on the board. Ask a student to come up and underline the verb forms. 1 and 4 have two forms, including the verb 'to be' as an auxiliary plus the past participle of the main verb. Sentences 2 and 3 only have the main verb in the past tense. Label auxiliary verbs, past participles and past tense forms clearly on the board using different colours.

Remind students that the active voice is the more common form and used when the subject does the action. The passive is used when the action is done to the subject, so this is less common. Not all verbs can be used in the passive voice.

1 passive	2 active	3 active	4 passive

14 Give students time to do the exercise individually. Have different students come to the board to write their answers. If they make any errors, elicit the correct answers from other students.

> 2 Trees were planted in the recreation area.
> 3 The bus stop was moved.
> 4 A new main reception was built.

EXAM SKILLS

15 Ask students to look at the floor plans. Check they know all the vocabulary. A gallery is typically where art is displayed. Ask students what changes have occurred. Students write their essays individually in class or for homework.

> *Sample answer*
> The maps show the changes to Colwick Arts Centre between 2005 and the present day. We can see that the Centre expanded and new facilities were added during this period.
>
> One of the major changes is that the outside area was developed. In 2005 there was an empty area of land outside the Centre. Trees were planted there and an outdoor exhibition area was made. The café was moved to the front of the Arts Centre and tables were added outside.
>
> Inside, a central exhibition area was created. The information desk was moved to the front of the central area. In the past there were two galleries but now there is only one; however, a drama studio was built. In 2005 the concert hall and cinema were in the same space, whereas now they are separate. In addition, an extra meeting room was constructed. The toilets moved to the opposite side of the Centre.
>
> So, it is clear that Colwick Arts Centre is more attractive today and has better facilities than in 2005.

Alternative

Students write their essays in pairs.

Feedback

Tell students what the focus of your feedback will be before you set the task. Tell them you will focus on the use of prepositions, verbs of change and the use of past tenses and the passive voice. When all the essays have been received, read out some which have a clear overview or particularly good use of the features you were focusing on.

LISTENING

> **OUTCOMES**
>
> • answer short-answer questions
> • spell names correctly.

OUTCOMES

Students may not know that spelling is important in the Listening test. If the spelling of a word is wrong, the mark is not given. Also, they are given a name to spell in Section 1, so they need to be able to write a word that is spelt out to them. This unit practises the exam skill of writing short answers to questions.

LEAD-IN

Students do exercises 01 and 02 in pairs.

01

A sports centre	B museum	C bank
D railway station	E bus stop	F restaurant
G harbour		

02

> Travel and Transport: bus stop, railway station
> Sports and leisure: sports centre, restaurant
> Arts and culture: museum
> Money: bank

Alternative

For a stronger class, put the students into two teams. Ask a student from each team to come to the board. Say one of the words from the box. The two students race to write it correctly on the board.

03 After students identify where the speakers are, ask them for the 'clues' that helped.

Transcript 15

Conversation 1

Man:	Good morning, how can I help you?
Woman:	Hello, I'd like some information about your facilities.
Man:	OK, well we have a swimming pool, squash courts, a gym and we have a couple of outdoor tennis courts too. You may have seen them on the left as you came in. Now, our website tells you how you can become a member and how much the yearly fee is. Do you want to make a note of the address?

Conversation 2

Bank clerk:	Good afternoon, can I help you?
Customer:	I'd like to open a new account please.
Bank clerk:	Certainly – now, is it a basic account you're looking to open or a savings account?
Customer:	A savings account.

Bank clerk:	Right – we can complete your application on line. I'll just get the form up on screen now. It won't take long.

1 sports centre	2 bank

After doing exercises 04 and 05, you might want to spend some time checking that your students are able to say and understand the alphabet, particularly the vowels e and I which are often confused. Listen out for the particular problems your students have with pronouncing letters and spend some time modelling the correct pronunciation and getting students to practise.

Transcript 16

Conversation 1

Man:	Good morning, how can I help you?
Woman:	Hello, I'd like some information about your facilities.
Man:	OK, well we have a swimming pool, squash courts, a gym and we have a couple of outdoor tennis courts too. You may have seen them on the left as you came in. Now, our website tells you how you can become a member and how much the yearly fee is. Do you want to make a note of the address?
Woman:	Oh, yes, please. I'll just put it on my phone now.
Man:	OK, it's W W W dot getactive.com. That's G-E-T-A-C-T-I-V-E dot com.
Woman:	'Get active' – is that all one word?
Man:	Yes, that's right.
Woman:	OK, I've got that. Thanks very much for your help.

Conversation 2

Bank clerk:	Good afternoon, can I help you?
Customer:	I'd like to open a new account, please.
Bank clerk:	Certainly – now, is it a basic account you're looking to open or a savings account?
Customer:	A savings account.
Bank clerk:	Right, we can complete your application on line. I'll just get the form up on screen now. It won't take long. So, I just need a few personal details. Can you give me your full name, please?
Customer:	James Clarke.
Bank clerk:	So, is that Clark with an 'e' or without?
Customer:	It's got an 'e' at the end. C-L-A-R-K-E.
Bank clerk:	And where do you live? What's your address?
Customer:	2 Waddington Road.
Bank clerk:	Can you spell that for me?
Customer:	That's W-A-double D-I-N-G-T-O-N Road.
Bank clerk:	Is that Waddington with a double D, did you say?
Customer:	That's right.
Bank clerk:	OK, so I just need a little more information about …

1 all one word	2 with	3 end	4 double

Extension

Students work in pairs to dictate their full name, address, telephone number and email address to each other. (Tell them they can make this up if they prefer).

06 Students should already be familiar with the term 'key words'. Elicit the definition before asking them to underline the key words in the questions.

> 2 How much did each person pay for their meal?
> 3 What time is the bus due?
> 4 Where is the bus stop?
> 5 How long did the course last?
> 6 Which TWO things did the speaker do on the course?
> 7 What is the date of the next course?
> 8 Who will lead the course?

07 The purpose of this exercise is to prepare students for the note completion task. Students may be more familiar with the questions. In the note completion task, they will just have a key word such as 'date' or 'name'.

> a date – 7
> a price – 2
> a period of time – 5
> a time – 3
> a meal or a kind of food – 1
> a name of a person – 8
> the names of activities or skills – 6
> a place – 4

08

Questions 2, 3, 5, 7

09 After the students have listened to the recording, point out that the correct answer ($20) was not the only number mentioned. There will often be other numbers to ensure students have understood the whole meaning and not just the number.

Transcript 18

A:	I really enjoyed that little place we went to last weekend – there was a really good choice of meat and fish, wasn't there?
B:	Did you really think so? I wish I could say the same, but actually, I thought it was pretty limited. There were far too many fish dishes on the menu and I can't stand seafood. There just wasn't enough meat.
A:	Oh, come on Jo! We really enjoyed the steak we had, and you said that the beef the people on the other table were eating looked delicious too.
B:	Well, I won't be going back. It was much too expensive.

A: Well, I thought it was pretty reasonable. In fact I couldn't believe it when the bill arrived. £40, including a tip. That's only £20 per person. You can't get steak for less than £15 anywhere in town.

1 steak	2 20

10-11 These exercises make students aware that they may still get the answer wrong even if they understand the recording. Make sure you stress the tips given here as they refer to common errors: not reading the instructions carefully and spelling mistakes.

10

'Shoes' is correct – 'he bought shoes' is three words, and the question asked for 'no more than one word and/or a number'.

Transcript 19

David: Hi, Leila! Where are you? We need to leave for the party soon.

Leila: I'm on my way home – I'm still waiting for the bus. I was going to get a taxi back but I've just checked my phone and there's one due in about fifteen minutes – seven fifty pm to be exact. And it seems to be running on time. It left the railway station a couple of minutes ago, so it's not too far away.

David: Do you want me to pick you up? I've got the car, so it's no problem. Where's the bus stop exactly?

Leila: It's the one on Blythe Road.

David: Blythe Road? I'm just checking it on my phone. Is that B-L-Y-T-H?

Leila: There's an e at the end of Blythe.

David: Got it. OK, I won't be long.

Leila: Actually, David – no need to pick me up – the traffic lights have just changed and I can see the bus coming now. I'd better go – I'll see you at home in a few minutes.

11

1 7.50 is the correct answer; 'seven fiftty' is incorrect because it is spelled wrong; 7.15 / seven fifteen is not the correct time.

2 Blythe Road

12 Ask students how many words they can write for each answer. After they have finished, point out the paraphrase they needed to understand for question 2 (the first thing Alicia learnt/the instructor began by teaching us. For question 4, ask students to spell the name back to you.

Transcript 20

Darren: Hi there, Alicia! How was your weekend? You were on a sailing course down at the harbour, weren't you?

Alicia: That's right – I really enjoyed breathing in all that fresh sea air. It was only two days but the time flew by! The instructor began by teaching us safety rules, which was necessary, but not very exciting. But then on the first morning we learnt how to open the sails and I even learned how to turn the boat. The water wasn't as calm as it looked, I can tell you – I lost my balance a few times!

Darren: Sounds like you had a lot of fun. I'd love to learn to sail.

Alicia: Well, there are plenty of courses and I think they run them once a month – so just let me check the website here. OK, so this was my course here – see – 4th and 5th of August. Now you could sign up for the next one, at the beginning of September. And it looks like there are still some spaces available.

Darren: So, the next one starts on 1st of September? I think I could do that.

Alicia: Well, let me give you the name of the course leader so that you can give him a call. He's a really experienced sailor ... OK, it's Jon Galloway.

Darren: Is that the usual spelling of John – J-O-H-N?

Alicia: No, there's no 'H' – he's just Jon, J-O-N.

Darren: OK, got you. And did you say his surname's Galloway? Can you spell that for me?

Alicia: Yes – Galloway – that's G-A-double L-O-W-A-Y. And I've got his number too. Why don't you give him a ring?

1 two/2 days	2 safety rules
3 1st (of) September / 1 September	4 Jon Galloway

Advice

When feeding back on listening exercises, refer students to examples of paraphrase as recognising different ways of expressing the same idea is a key skill in the Listening test.

EXAM SKILLS

13-15 If possible, check each student's answers to ensure they have followed the instructions and have the correct spellings. If your class is too big, ask students to check each other's' answers.

13

You need to write a number only for questions 3 and 5.

14

1 What kind of tour did the woman do?
2 How did she find out about the tour?
3 How many people were on the tour?
4 What is the address of the hire shop?
5 How much did each student in the group pay?
6–7 Which TWO items were included in the cost of the hire?
8 What is the website address of the hire shop?

Transcript 21

Jon: So, how's your very first week at university going, Rita? It's Orientation Week for you all new students, isn't it?

Rita: Yes, that's right – Orientation Week. Yes, it's great fun – there are so many different events going on to help us make friends and find our way around the university. And to get around the city, come to that! But you'll remember all that, Jon. You were a new student once!

Jon: That's true. I remember I went on a walking tour of the city on my very first day. And I think some students did a bus tour.

Rita: Well I did a bike tour – I was sent an email about it and I decided to sign up. There were only eight places and there were seven other names on the list already, so I got the very last place.

Jon: I didn't know you had a bike.

Rita: I *don't* have a bike but that didn't matter. We all hired them – from a little cycle hire shop on Barkway Street. You probably know the place.

Jon: Barclay Street? Do you mean the 'Barclay Street' on campus?

Rita: No, it's Barkway Street – B-A-R-K-W-A-Y. Number 22 Barkway Street, to be exact. It was great – we could choose a traditional bike or an electric one.

Jon: So, I take it you went electric!

Rita: Yes, of course I did! Well, think about it – why ride a traditional bike when you can get around the city much faster on an electric one! And because there was a group of us, it wasn't too expensive. In fact the cycle hire was only a hundred and twenty dollars for the whole group. So the cost was only fifteen dollars per person and that was for three whole hours!

Jon: Did you say fifty dollars?

Rita: No, fifteen dollars. So I thought it was really quite cheap. And I didn't have to bring along a helmet to wear either. That was included – and we also got a lock, so it was easy to park our bikes safely when we wanted to stop and take a break!

Jon: Sounds good. Have you got the website address of the place you got your bike from? I quite like the idea of doing a bike tour.

Rita: Yes – it's a really easy one to remember. It's tradelectric.com

Jon: Can you say that again?

Rita: tradelectric – T-R-A-D-E-L-E-C-T-R-I-C all one word dot com.

Jon: Thanks, Rita.

Rita: No problem. Hey, maybe we can do a bike tour together. I'd love to cycle as far as the harbour next time.

Jon: Great! That's a date then!

15

1 bike/cycle/cycling (tour)	2 (by) email
3 eight/8	4 22 Barkway Street
5 fifteen/15 (dollars)	6 helmet/lock
7 lock/helmet	8 tradelectric.com

SPEAKING

OUTCOMES

- use prepositions to talk about your home town
- use adjectives to describe your home town
- use the correct tense when responding to questions
- pronounce regular and irregular past simple tense endings.

OUTCOMES

The speaking test begins with students being asked either about their home/home town or their work/studies. Therefore, it is essential that all students can talk about these effectively. All the outcomes of this lesson focus on helping students talk accurately about their home town.

LEAD-IN

01 The aim of this exercise is to ensure students can name the tenses and are aware that they will be asked questions in different tenses in the speaking test. Avoid going into detail of the form and use of the tenses here.

1 B	2 C	3 A

02 Students work in pairs to ask and answer the questions. Circulate and correct any errors you hear immediately.

Alternative

For a weaker class, model the answers for your own town.

03 If necessary, check all students know the meanings of the vocabulary in the box.

Ideally students label the map as they listen. Allow them a few minutes to complete it by reading if necessary.

A cinema B art gallery C shopping mall D harbour
E stadium F swimming pool G library H town hall

Transcript 22

Boy: Well, I live in a small town in the north of my country. It has quite a few interesting places to visit. For example, in the centre of town, on the north side of the square we have the historic town hall, which was built in 1895. In front of it, there's a beautiful fountain. Opposite the town hall there's the library. Then if you go over the bridge, we have the art gallery, a big modern building, which often has interesting exhibitions. The art gallery is actually between the cinema (to the north) and a big shopping mall, where I o en meet up with my friends.

To the south of the town, there's a harbour, where you can take a boat to the islands. And then next to the harbour is the stadium, where people go to watch our local football team. And just behind it is the public swimming pool. It's an outdoor pool – lovely in summer, but very chilly the rest of the year.

Advice

Listening with the script is a useful activity to do occasionally as it helps students see the connection between spoken and written forms of the language. However, most listening should be done without the script to prepare students for the exam and real listening contexts.

Extension

Ask students to cover the script and explain where the items in the box are located using their completed maps.

04 Ask students to draw a quick map of either the centre of their home town or the area where they live. Working in pairs, they describe their map to their partner, who tries to recreate it from the description. Make sure they don't look at each other's maps.

05 Before students start this activity, ask them which adjectives they have heard or used in the lesson so far.

Students work in pairs to do exercises 5, 6 and 7. Allow dictionaries if needed. Point out that some of the items in the 'Location' column are phrases rather than isolated words.

2 Opinion	3 Climate	4 Areas
5 Buildings		

06

Opinion:	colourful, incredible, magnificent, polluted
Climate:	cool
Location:	in the south, indoor
Areas:	tourist
Buildings:	ancient, narrow, enormous, high-rise, huge

07

1 tall and high-rise	2 hot and humid
3 cool and mild	4 dirty and polluted
5 lively and exciting	

Advice

It is a good idea to remind students regularly that words should be learnt as part of a phrase or in conjunction with other words they are often used with.

Extension

Ask students if the sentences in exercise 7 are true for their city. If not, can they think of other pairs that would suit their city?

08 This exercise provides 'freer practice' of the vocabulary they have practised in previous exercises. Allow the students plenty of time to do this, working with a partner. If they discover new words, make sure they make a note of them.

08

Possible adjectives

1 huge, incredible, magnificent, busy, crowded, exciting

2 ancient, flat, outdoor, narrow, historic, quiet

3 hot, humid, crowded, narrow, flat, exciting, lively, colourful

GRAMMAR FOCUS: TENSES

09 Read the tip to the students. Check they understand 'echo'. Point out that this can also give them thinking time. Ask why they should not do it too often. If they are not sure, tell them it would not be natural or might make the examiner think they don't understand much.

1 past simple	2 present simple	3 present perfect

10 Tell students to read through the whole dialogue before starting to answer as this will help them understand the context.

Transcript 23

Examiner	Where were you born?
Candidate 1	I was born in Dubai, in the Middle East. It is situated on the north-east coast of the United Arab Emirates.

2

Examiner	Where did you grow up?
Candidate 2	I was born in a small village in China, but I grew up in Chengdu, which is a very big city in south-west China.

3

Examiner	Has your home town changed much since you were a child?
Candidate 3	In the last ten years Baku has changed a lot. Ten years ago we didn't have so many tall buildings and there wasn't as much to do then. The biggest problem is that everything's more expensive now.

4

Examiner	Is there anything that you used to do in your home town that you don't do now?
Candidate 4	Well, I used to go to the beach every summer when I was younger, but now I don't have time. One summer, I even went fishing. I'd like to do that again. Perhaps I'll have time next summer, after my exams.

1 was	2 is	3 was	4 grew up
5 is	6 has changed	7 didn't have	8 wasn't
9 is	10 used to	11 was	12 went

'I was born' often poses particular problems for students so you might want to highlight this in some way, e.g. by having all the students say where they were born.

Check meaning of 'used to'- I did it in the past but don't now.

Extension

After checking their answers, students can practise reading the dialogues in pairs.

11 Refer students back to the vocabulary they learnt in the Writing section, which might be useful when explaining how their city has changed.

12 When checking this exercise, ensure students are aware that some verbs gain an extra syllable in the past tense (e.g. situate-situated, locate-located). Students often lack confidence in pronouncing these words.

> /t/ bought, built, developed, used to
> /d/ called, changed, designed, discovered, said
> /id/ situated, located, started

13 Tell students to use their imagination for this exercise. It does not have to be true of their own home town.

Transcript 24

1	Our family bought an apartment in the middle of town.
2	The statue was built in 1985.
3	Our town is situated on the Yangtze river.
4	The shopping mall is called 'the Galleria'.
5	The library is located across from the swimming pool.
6	Many things have changed over the years in my home town.
7	A number of new apartments were developed by the harbour.
8	The bridge was designed by a famous architect from London.
9	Recently, scientists discovered a large cave near our village.
10	Recently, many young people have started to leave my hometown to look for work.
11	A long time ago many people used to work in factories in my town.
12	A tourist who visited recently said our town is a great place to visit.

14 After checking students' answers, ask them how they matched the questions and answers.

Get students to find a different partner to work with to ask and answer the questions.

Transcript 25

Speaker 1: In my city there are a lot of things that people can do to enjoy themselves. I personally enjoy visiting the many parks we have, but only in summer when the weather is fine. In winter, people like to visit the cinema or sometimes it's possible to go ice skating on the lake.

Speaker 2: Well, I'm really keen on sport, especially swimming. I live in quite a small town, so we only have one swimming pool and I spend as much time as I can there, when I'm not studying of course!

Speaker 3: Most of the city is pretty modern, but there's an ancient castle where the Emperor used to live. It's just a place for tourists to visit now, but in the past it was the most important place in the country and it's over 1000 years old.

Speaker 4: It depends, there are a lot of traffic jams in the morning and evening when everybody is going to work or school, but the public transport is very modern and the underground's fast and cheap.

> Speaker 1 –b   Speaker 2 –a   Speaker 3 –d
> Speaker 4 –c

EXAM SKILLS

15 Ask students to read through the questions and ask you if there are any questions they are not sure of. Where possible, pair students with someone from a different town or a different part of town. Give plenty of time for both students to give full answers to all 8 questions.

Feedback

Students can give each other feedback when you are not able to listen to all students. Ask students to listen for errors in use of tenses and note them down to tell the speaker at the end. Ask them to listen out for speakers' use of new vocabulary too.

Ask students if they feel confident about describing their home town. If they are not, tell them you will provide more practice in a future lesson.

READING

OUTCOMES

- identify the main ideas of a passage
- find information in a text quickly
- deal with multiple-choice questions.

OUTCOMES

Several of the task types in the Reading paper require students to identify main ideas. Students will need to read the texts to find specific information in order to locate answers to questions. In this unit students will learn some techniques to help them with scanning in general and in particular to handle Multiple Choice Questions.

Scanning

Moving your eyes across a text to find specific information, ignoring everything that is not relevant.

LEAD-IN

01 The IELTS speaking test starts with students either being asked about their home (which they looked at in Units 1 and 2) or their work/studies which they will look at in this unit. Questions related to these topics are also common in the writing paper.

Students work in pairs to put the words into one of two categories. They can use dictionaries, if necessary.

Don't explain meanings at this stage as students will have the opportunity to work out meanings from the context.

Work: business, employers, job, office, retirement

Studies: academic, blended learning, degree, lifelong learning, primary education, qualification, seminars

02 This is an opportunity to practise scanning skills. If appropriate, this can be a race.

The next few exercises will guide students through the process as outlined in the information box on Multiple Choice questions. As they do these exercises, link them clearly to the stages in the box.

All the words except *office* are in the text.

03 This is a 'gist' question.

Gist

The main idea of a text, not the detail. We usually skim read to find the gist.

Make sure you enforce the time limit. If students say they have not finished reading in one minute, tell them they do not have time to read the whole text in detail. If they have not finished, they may not have adopted the right reading style.

The text is more positive than negative.

Ask how they identified that the text is mainly positive.

04 The aim of this exercise is to help students identify which part of the text contains the answer. At this stage, they are not trying to find the answer, just the relevant paragraph.

Students need to identify the key words in the sentence stem before reading the options.

Sentence stem

The beginning of a sentence that is to be completed by choosing one of the options.

For question 1, they need to search for 'blended learning'- a synonym is unlikely to be used here; for question 2 they need to search either for 'advantages' 'and 'globalised education' or their synonyms.

Students should be able to locate the actual sentence stem, 'blended learning means' in paragraph A. However, they will have to identify paraphrase to find the correct option. The texts defines blended learning as 'studying partly in a traditional way in the classroom and partly online or via email', which is a paraphrase of option C.

In question 2, point out that the word 'elite' in option D is defined in the text. Even without that, there is another clue as the idea of the elite getting the opportunities is introduced at the beginning of Paragraph C with the words 'it is not good news for everyone'

1 C (Para A) You only need to read part of the paragraph (*studying partly in a traditional way in the classroom and partly online or via email*).

2 D (Paras B and C) You need to read the whole of paragraph B and the beginning of C. The elite having most of the opportunities is not a benefit.

Advice

It is worth pointing out this kind of example to students to reassure them that not knowing a word in the question is not always a problem.

05 The aim of this exercise is to help students predict which words might be paraphrased in a text. We have already seen the example of 'blended learning' which is a technical term. Similarly, the terms 'globalisation', 'distance learning', 'lifelong learning' and 'westernisation' are specific terms which will probably not be paraphrased.

1 overseas	2 advantages	3 disrupting
4 attending	5 enrich	6 valuable
7 offices		

06 Tell students that the practice of 'sampling' the text can be a way to identify main ideas.

Sampling a text

Read the first and last paragraphs and the first sentence of every paragraph in between. This gives you a good chance of quickly identifying the main ideas.

Ask students to 'sample' the text and identify the four sentences which represent the main ideas.

The topic sentence is often but not always the first. It can also be the second or last sentence in a paragraph.

Sentences 1, 3, 4, 6. The main ideas can usually be found in the first sentence of the paragraph.

Extension

Ask students to decide if the topic sentence is the first sentence in the paragraphs in this text.

07 There is not always just one correct way to answer questions in IELTS. Students can try out different ways and use the one that works for them. In this approach, students answer the questions as if there were no options and then link their answer to one of the options.

Encourage students to try this for themselves. Point out that students do not have to adopt just one approach. They can switch between approaches depending on the question.

1 **B**   2 **A**   3 **C**

GRAMMAR FOCUS: THE PRESENT PERFECT

08 The Reading exercises aim to highlight how students' awareness of grammar can help them to understand the text. Point out that several of the paragraphs in the text start with a Present Perfect sentence to highlight the links between past and present and then switch to the Simple Present as the writer's focus is on the current situation.

1 The sentences all relate to the present and the past.

  a The level was raised in the past and is still high in the present.

  b They were not educated in the past, which affects their present.

  c They became businesses in the past and they are still businesses.

2 b

3 a

EXAM SKILLS

09 Draw students' attention to the information box, which reminds them of the approach to answering MCQs practised in the unit.

Alternative

Students try to answer the questions without the options and then find the option which most closely matches their own answer. They could use different approaches on different questions, and decide which one works best for them.

1 B   2 C   3 D   4 A

WRITING

OUTCOMES

- describe different types of data
- describe changes in numbers
- use prepositions with numbers.

OUTCOMES

This unit introduces the students to the four main types of chart used in Writing Task 1, as well as developing their skills in describing numbers. Point out that many tasks present changes to data over time, and they will need to be able to describe them with some precision.

LEAD-IN

01 The examples represent data which show changes over time as well as data which do not.

1 line graph   2 pie chart   3 bar chart   4 table

1 and 4 describe changes to numbers over time.

02 Most of these words have the same form as nouns and verbs Point out that 'growth' is a noun and the verb is 'grow' (grew, grown).

↑	↓
increase (V, N)	fall (V, N)
rise (V, N)	drop (V, N)
growth (N)	decrease (V, N)
	decline (V, N)

03 Do 'fall' and 'increase' as examples with the class. Tell students that 'fall' is irregular (fell, fallen) and 'increase' is regular (increased, increased).

Students do the exercise in pairs. Point out the double 'p' in 'dropped'.

infinitive	past simple	past participle
fall	fell	fallen
increase	increased	increased
drop	dropped	dropped
decrease	decreased	decreased
decline	declined	declined
rise	rose	risen
grow	grew	grown

Extension

Students label the verbs as R (regular) or I (Irregular).

Check students can pronounce the past forms correctly.

04 This exercise gives students the chance to practise meaning and grammar in a controlled IELTS context.

Alternative

Before students complete the gaps, ask them whether the word needed is a noun or a verb.

1 rose
2 fall /drop/decline/decrease
3 rise / growth / increase
4 declined / decreased / fell / dropped OR have declined / have decreased / have fallen / have dropped

05 It is important to draw students' attention to the tip before they read the descriptions of the graph. The rubric of the exam tells students to 'select' information which is important. Ask students what kind of information might be (the highest, lowest, greatest change etc).

Ask students to start by looking at the graph and making some points about it. Elicit:

- A rising trend
- The rise is steady throughout the period
- The % of graduates has risen from about 17% to about 38%

This exercise is important because it shows that students are not meant to do what the writer of Paragraph A has done- i.e. mechanically recount all the information. The writer of Paragraph B has interpreted the data. Instead of mentioning the given figures, this writer has turned them into the percentage by which the number of graduates has increased. Since no period sticks out particularly, s/he has just given an example of the trend.

B is better because it gives an overview and summarises the data with an example. A is just a list of all the data.

06 Start by drawing students' attention to the graph rather than the sentences. Ask them some questions to make sure they understand the graph, e.g. What was the most popular activity for 18 year olds in 2014? Approximately how many students were in work-based learning?

There are two main purposes to this exercise. One is to make students aware that they must not include any outside information or any opinion on the data. The other is to emphasise that it is important to comment on salient features of the data. Therefore, while the answer to question 2 could be a matter of opinion, the sentences marked as 'most important' relate to salient data.

Salient features

Salient features are those that 'stick out' as being special in some way because they are the highest, lowest or different from other data in some way.

1 Sentences 2 and 7 should not be included.
2 Sentences 1, 6, 8 and 9 are probably the most important. (To some extent this is a matter of opinion, but the answer should include the highest and lowest numbers, for example.)

07 Emphasise the importance of prepositions generally and particularly those in these kind of number-related phrases. After the exercise is completed, highlight that prepositions can change the whole meaning of a sentence, e.g. It increased to 100./It increased by 100.

1 of	2 of, up	3 from, to	4 by	5 Between	6 in

Advice

Ask students to have a separate page in their vocabulary books for phrases with prepositions. They tend to underestimate the importance of these little words so it is a useful way of emphasising them.

08 Ask students to study the question and graph clearly and ensure they understand it before reading the model answer. The two groups are unemployed people in the age range 21-30. The group is divided into recent graduates and non-graduates. Before looking at the essay, try to elicit the following:

- Unemployment is higher among non-graduates at all points
- Both groups display similar trends
- The main trends are fall then rise
- There was a plateau among recent graduates between 2000 and 2020

Students read the model essay and find the features. If they have print copies, they can highlight the features in different colours.

Use this opportunity to remind students of the importance of the overview and having data to support the description.

1 The line graph shows the number of unemployed recent graduates and non-graduates in the population of 21 to 30-year-olds in the years between 1990 and 2015.

2 Overall, the numbers have not changed much: we can see a fall, followed by a rise, in both groups. The non-graduates are a larger number than the recent graduates at all points.

3 (*sample answer*) There was a small change in the middle period. / The number of non-graduates dropped and then grew during that period.

4 Over the five years from 2010 to 2015, the numbers of both non-graduates and recent graduates returned almost to their 1990 figures of 10 14 and 10%.

5 was, dropped, grew, returned

6 Overall, the numbers **have not changed** much

The past simple is used more because most of the verbs refer to actions completed in the past. The one example of the present perfect is used because it refers up to the present. (The text was written in 2015).

09 Ask students to study the pie chart for a minute. Point out that the numbers add up to 100 so it shows the proportion of 100 that each country represents. Ask students to talk about the pie chart in their own words to their partner. After they do the exercise, point out that these phrases will generally be useful for pie charts.

1 USA	2 UK	3 New Zealand	4 Canada
5 Australia	6 USA	7 UK	8 New Zealand

EXAM SKILLS

10 Students will practise writing a Task 1 with guidance. Tell them that the questions in exercise 10 are the kind of questions they should ask themselves whenever they do a Task 1 essay.

Check understanding of 'literacy'.

Depending on your class, you might want to have them answer the questions orally with a partner instead of writing them.

Make sure students know they are to write an essay and not a list of answers to the questions.

Students write the essay in class or for homework.

1 grey – male, purple – female
2 vertical – percentage of people who are literate; horizontal – region of the world
3 Central Asia, Central/Eastern Europe
4 five
5 South and West Asia
6 male – about 70%, female – about 59% (Sub-Saharan Africa)
7 male – about 30%, female – about 41%

11 Students write their answer taking into account the previous advice.

Feedback

You could prepare a tick-box feedback sheet for the essay, for example:

	YES	NO	To some extent
Introductory sentence			
Overview			
Correct use of past tense forms			
Accurate description of trends			
Data to support description			

Make sure students have time to study your feedback on their essay. If possible, get them to rewrite it, taking into account your feedback.

11

Sample answer

The data shows the literacy rate for both males and females in seven different regions of the world. The horizontal axis lists the regions and the vertical axis shows percentage. In all regions except two, there is a difference in the literacy rates of men and women.

Central Asia and Central/Eastern Europe have the highest percentage of citizens who can read and write. Almost 100% of men and women are literate in those regions. The lowest literacy rates are in Sub-Saharan Africa.

In five out of the seven regions, there are different literacy rates for men and women. The greatest difference between men and women is found in South and West Asia. In this region, about 80% of men are able to read and write, but only about 60% of women. Overall, the difference between the most literate area and the least literate is about 30% for men and just over 40% for women.

In conclusion, literacy rates vary between regions, with males having higher levels than females in most regions. (171 words)

LISTENING

OUTCOMES

- identify key words in sentence completion tasks
- use strategies to help you answer sentence completion tasks
- follow a conversation
- recognise synonyms and paraphrase.

OUTCOMES

Get students to read the outcomes.

> **Strategies**
>
> A detailed plan for how to approach a task in order to achieve success.

They will have noticed that the words 'synonyms' and 'paraphrase' come up in all parts of the test so they really are key concepts in IELTS. This unit will also further develop their vocabulary in relation to the topic.

LEAD-IN

01 Students match the words and pictures in pairs. Ensure students can pronounce all the words correctly.

A construction	B sports and leisure
C retail	D hotel and catering
E health	F art and design
G information technology	

Exercises 02 to 04 help students differentiate between similar words. Read the Tip with them before they attempt the exercises. Understanding that certain suffixes relate to particular parts of speech can help them avoid some of the common errors in the listening test.

02
badminton coach J   building engineering C
chef J   computing C   doctor J   fitness training C
food technology C   graphic designer J   medicine C
shop management C   store assistant J   textiles C
web designer J

03
1 graphic designer ... textiles
2 architect ... building engineering
3 doctor ... medicine
4 chef ... food technology
5 web designer ... computing
6 store assistant ... shop management
7 badminton coach ... fitness training

04
1 computing, food technology   2 chef, doctor
3 architect, store assistant   4 fitness training, textiles

05 After students do the exercise, ask them what clues in the text helped them.

Transcript 26

Conversation 1

Manager: Come on in. It's Anna, isn't it?

Anna: Yes, that's right. Anna Scott.

Manager: Ah yes. Take a seat, Anna. First of all, we're delighted that you'll be joining us as a store assistant at the beginning of next week.

Anna: Thanks very much. I'm really looking forward to the challenge.

Manager: That's good to know.

Conversation 2

Receptionist: Good morning, you're through to Milton College. How can I help?

Student: Oh, hello there. I'd like to book a place on the Food Photography course.

Receptionist: OK. Now, is that the one that starts on the 18th?

Student: No, that's the date of the Food *Technology* course – I want the Food *Photography* course. It's the day after.

Receptionist: OK ... got it right up on screen now. Food Photography – Saturday 19th of September. And it looks like you're in luck – there are only a couple of spaces left. We've taken ten bookings already, so you've just made it – the course is limited to twelve participants. It's very popular.

Student: That's good to know! Now can I just check the details of the course?

Conversation 1: J	Conversation2: C

06 Underlining the words before or after the gaps helps students identify the type of word that is needed. For example the word 'a' before a gap tells them that a noun beginning with a consonant sound is needed.

Students should also underline the key words in the questions.

1 Anna has got a job as a _____ .
2 She has recently completed a course in _____ .
3 The new name of the department which sells computers and phones is _____ .
4 The course takes place on the _____ of September.
5 There is a total of _____ places available on the course.

07 This exercise prepares students for the prediction they will need to do in all parts of the listening test. They should use the preparation time given before each section of the test to predict what type of information they will need.

an area of study – 2	a type of job – 1
a number only – 5	a name of a place – 3
a date – 4	

08 These short exercises are a good chance to instil in students the need to check the instructions carefully for the number of words needed and to check the grammar carefully.

Transcript 27

Manager: Come on in. It's Anna, isn't it?

Anna: Yes, that's right. Anna Scott.

Manager:	Ah yes. Take a seat, Anna. First of all, we're delighted that you'll be joining us as a store assistant at the beginning of next week.
Anna:	Thanks very much. I'm really looking forward to the challenge.
Manager:	That's good to know. Now, we know you've just finished a course in Information Technology, so we've decided to put you in the computing and phones section of our department store.
Anna:	That's great. Now, that's next to the radios and audio equipment, isn't it?
Manager:	That's right. All our radios and audio are in a part of the store we used to call the 'Sound Station'. But as I've just said, you'll be based in the computing and phones section. Now we've recently made this area of our store much bigger so that we can sell a much wider range of computer equipment, such as smart watches.
Anna:	Mm. Smart watches.
Manager:	Yes, we really want to attract a younger group of customers. And we haven't just given this whole area a completely new look – we've re-named it too!
Anna:	Re-named it?
Manager:	Yes. From next week it's going to be known as 'Moving Images'.
Anna:	'Moving Images'? Cool! I like it.
Manager:	Now, do you have any questions before we move on?

> 1 store assistant 2 information technology
> 3 Moving Images

09 This exercise draws students' attention to some common errors that students make including not checking that the word they've written matches a/an before the gap, and confusing singular and plural forms.

> 1 store assistant (it can't be *assistant* because the word before is 'a' not 'an')
>
> 2 information technology (*informations* is incorrect as a plural form – the word *information* is uncountable)
>
> 3 Moving Images (The Moving Images consists of three words and the instructions tell you to use no more than two words. Moving Image is incorrect because it is singular, and the speaker uses the plural.)

10 This is another chance to stress that students need to check instructions carefully. Draw their attention to the wording 'AND/OR'. Ask can they write a word AND a number?-Yes.

The tip also focuses on a common error, which is that students write words or symbols that are already in the sentence. If the sentence reads, for example, There are a total of 12 places places available on the course' it will be marked wrong.

> 1 19th [of] / nineteenth [of]   2 12 / twelve

11 The answers with 'Sept' or 'September' are wrong because the word September is in the sentence. After 'the' we would say '19th' not '19'. There is a spelling mistake too (ninteenth), which serves to reinforce the Tip- it is easy to make mistakes when spelling out the whole word.

> The correct answers are: 19, 19th, nineteenth of

12 This exercise encourages students to use the questions themselves to help them follow the conversation.

> a the price of the course – 6
> b the location of the course – 5
> c the name of the course – 1
> d the starting time of the course – 2
> e the purpose of the course – 4
> f the duration of the course – 3

13 Point out here that the words in this exercise are used quite frequently in listening section 1

Extension

If students have not already done so, this would be a good chance for them to start a 'synonyms and antonyms' section in their vocabulary notebook.

> 1 h 2 i 3 f 4 e 5 d 6 c 7 b 8 a 9 g

EXAM SKILLS

14-16 Before doing the practice activity, elicit from students what they have learnt in this lesson. Refer them to the checklist in exercise 16 before they listen.

Extension

Students can make a copy of this checklist in their notebooks to use when they do other listening activities of this kind.

Transcript 28

Student:	Now can I just check the details of the course?
Receptionist:	Sure, go ahead.
Student:	Now it says on the leaflet … um, let me find it … OK, got it! Right, so it's called Food Photography, and I've got here that it begins at nine thirty.
Receptionist:	That's right – it's an early start. It begins at half past nine and it goes on until four thirty. Most of our weekend courses are quite short and so they're over in a couple of hours – this course is longer. According to the information I've got up here on screen, it's seven hours long.

Student:	Oh, I'm glad it lasts for more than a few hours. I don't think I'd be able to learn how to take good pictures in *less* than seven hours.
Receptionist:	Now I'll just give you a bit more information about the course itself. Basically, you'll learn how to take good photos of food using a digital camera. So it'll train you in the basics of using a range of camera angles.
Student:	Camera angles?
Receptionist:	Yes, you'll learn how to photograph food using close-up shots, wide angle shots and shots taken from above, that sort of thing.
Student:	What about learning to edit pictures on my computer? Will that be covered too?
Receptionist:	No, I'm afraid not. The purpose of the workshop is to teach you how to take good photos in the first place. It's a really hands-on session – in fact, you'll spend some of the day on location in a local hotel. It's just round the corner from the college – the Lincoln Hotel – so you'll have the opportunity to practise taking photographs using real dishes!
Student:	That's great – a practical course is exactly what I'm looking for!
Receptionist:	Now just a few more things. The full fee of the course is $55 and that includes a light lunch and refreshments at the hotel.
Student:	Oh, that's really good. That means I don't have to worry about bringing along my own drinks and snacks on the day. That would probably cost me at least ten dollars.
Receptionist:	OK, I think that's everything, so I'll just take your details so that we can confirm your place on the course.

14

1 title – it's called	2 starts – begins
3 lasts – goes on	4 teach – train
5 part – some; nearby – local	6 total cost – full fee

15

1 Food Photography	2 9.30 / nine thirty [am]
3 7 / seven	4 camera angles
5 hotel	6 $55 / fifty-five dollars

SPEAKING

OUTCOMES

- answer simple questions about your work and studies (Speaking Part 1)
- use some strategies to prepare for a talk (Speaking Part 2)
- introduce your talk (Speaking Part 2)
- pronounce words beginning with two consonants.

OUTCOMES

This lesson will cover aspects of both Part 1 and Part 2 of the speaking test.

LEAD-IN

01 Students work in pairs to match the words and pictures.

A emergency services*	B travel and transport
C farming	D education
E tourism	F science research and development
G entertainment	

* the organizations that deal with accidents and urgent problems such as fire, illness or crime

> **Extension**
>
> Ask students to discuss in pairs which areas they would/ would not like to work in and why. Refer them to exercise 2. Some of the words might help them express their ideas.

02 Give an example of words with a negative meaning- e.g. sad. Elicit the opposite of negative, i.e. positive. Write positive and negative on the board. Give students time to do the exercise. Have students come to the board and write the words into the columns.

tired, boring, embarrassed, not very exciting,

03 Ask students if you can say 'I feel tired'-Yes. Can you say 'I feel boring'-No. Students do the exercise in pairs. If they have difficulty with this, don't worry. Exercise 4 will clarify it.

amazed F	boring E	challenging E
embarrassed F	fascinated F	great F, E
interesting E	not very exciting E	thrilled F tired F

04 Write the sentence stems on the board:

I feel/felt..   It is/It was…

amazed   amazing

Write an example in each column with the suffixes in a different colour, as above.

'Great' is different from the other words. It doesn't end in 'ed' or 'ing' and can refer both to feelings and experience.

I feel / I felt ...	It is / It was
thrilled	thrilling
bored	boring
challenged	challenging
fascinated	fascinating
not very excited	not very exciting
tired	tiring
embarrassed	embarrassing
interested	interesting
great	great

05 This exercise puts the vocabulary from the previous exercises into context. You might want to get students to do this individually to check they understand both the meaning and the grammar.

1 thrilled	2 interesting	3 embarrassed
4 bored	5 tiring	6 amazing

Extension

Ask students to tell you about a time they have felt bored, thrilled, excited, embarrassed, interested, amazed, etc and an experience that was boring, thrilling, exciting, embarrassing, interesting, amazing etc.

Their responses will help you check their understanding.

06 Make sure students have the vocabulary to describe the activities. The students practise using present perfect and simple

SPEAKING TEST – PART 1

07-08 This tip is very important. Students don't have to tell the truth at all times in the speaking test. They just have to answer the question. They will listen to the recording twice, once for gist and once to order the information.

Transcript 29

Examiner:	What do you do? Do you work or are you a student?
Miriam:	I'm a student. I'm doing a part-time fashion and textiles course. I'm at Milton College, in the centre of the city. I'm in my third year and at the moment I'm studying twelve hours a week.
Examiner:	Are you enjoying it?
Miriam:	Oh yes, I am. I think it's great. I particularly like working with different materials like wool and leather. And I've just made a beautiful scarf and it's made out of plastic. It looks very strange but I think it's great! It's pretty amazing in fact!
Examiner:	Would you like to learn anything new in future?
Miriam:	Yes, I would. I'd really like to learn how to use computer software to create new designs. This should also help me create new shades of colour. Using technology in this way would be really challenging for me, I think.
Examiner:	And is there a job you would really like to do in the future?
Miriam:	Yes, there is. I'd love the chance to become a fashion photographer. And if I do well on my course and get some experience of taking pictures at my college fashion shows, perhaps my dream will come true. I've just bought myself a new digital camera and I've already learned how to take some great close-up shots!

07

> Photograph D; she's a student

08

> What job she would like to do in the future 6
>
> How many hours a week she studies/works 3
>
> What she does 1
>
> What she would like to learn in the future 5
>
> What she thinks about her studies/work 4
>
> Where she studies/works 3

09 This kind of exercise is a useful way of getting students talking as they don't have to make up new content- they use the prompts to say what they remember about Anna.

10 In the speaking test, students will only have 1 minute to prepare. Give them as much time as they need at this stage.

11 Make sure students have enough time for both partners to answer all questions.

Alternative

Students record their answers on their phone and self-evaluate their speech for homework.

12 Pronunciation is done in short slots in this book. However, whenever students do speaking activities, check their pronunciation of any problem areas.

SPEAKING TEST – PART 2

13 Part 2 tasks are quite personal and generally ask about a particular occasion, activity or plan the student has. Topic 1 is too general and large but might come up in Part 3. 5 and 6 might be asked in Part 1.

> Topics 2, 3, 4 are possible Part 2 topics.

14 This exercise familiarises students with Part 2. It is generally common sense.

Alternative

Show students a Part 2 from Youtube in order to help them complete exercise 14.

> The order is: E, C, D, A, B, F

15-16 These exercises focus on the preparation for Part 2. Making notes is not compulsory but it will help students remember to cover all the points.

15

> Describe a time when you <u>learned</u> something <u>new</u>
>
> You should say:
>
> - <u>what</u> you <u>learnt</u>
> - <u>how</u> you <u>learnt</u> it
> - <u>what</u> the <u>result</u> was
>   and <u>explain how you felt</u> about learning something new.

16

What?	learned to fly a small plane
How?	had lessons at a flying club
Result?	got my pilot's licence
How I felt?	thrilled and proud of myself

17 Using these introductory phrases will give student's confidence and thinking time. At this stage, they practise just the opening sentences with a partner.

18 This exercise helps students see the relationship between the student's notes and her talk so it should clarify for them why making notes is a good idea.

Transcript 31

Nina: I'm going to tell you about a time when I learned something new. What did I learn? Well, I've always been an active and sporty person and I really like cold weather – I love it when it snows in my country. That's why I decided to learn something that mixes these things together – winter, sport and snow! So, I decided to learn to ski!

I learned with an instructor. There was a big group of us – we had a great instructor. It was really exciting when we were on the chair lift on the first day. We started on the nursery slope – I couldn't even walk on my skis at first and I fell over many times. It took me a long time to learn how to keep my balance. It really is much more difficult than it looks! It was great fun! I really liked learning in a group – much better than learning individually.

In fact, I was in a skiing competition recently and I won! I got a silver cup. So, I think that's quite a good result.

How did I feel about the learning experience? Well, it was really thrilling to ski downhill for the very first time – I loved the feeling of speed. It was very exciting! I was so proud of myself when I reached the bottom of the slope and I was still standing! It was a great feeling!

Extension

Students read the audioscript and find words to describe feelings and experiences. Ask them to highlight any words and phrases that are new to them.

1 d	2 a	3 c	4 b

19 Allow students plenty of time to prepare their notes.

20 It will be quite difficult for students to talk for two minutes without hesitation at this stage. Don't expect too much. Let them practise in private in a corner of the classroom, any spare classrooms or hall space.

Feedback

Praise students for completing the task of speaking for 1 to 2 minutes. Focus on whether their notes were full enough to enable them to talk at length. What could they have added? Don't focus on errors at this stage. If students wish to record themselves doing the task, they can self-evaluate at home.

UNIT/04: FOOD AND DRINK

READING

> ### OUTCOMES
> - locate and match information from a text
> - complete gapped sentences
> - correct common errors in the use of countable/uncountable nouns
> - use *some, any, much* and *many*.

This unit gives further practice in the key IELTS skills of locating information quickly and understanding paraphrase. It particularly supports the task type where students have to match information to different categories. They also learn to complete sentences with a word from the text. For this they need to be aware of the part of speech of the missing word to make sure the sentence is grammatical. In this unit we focus on countable and uncountable nouns. Lack of awareness in this area can lead to mistakes with verb forms and articles, which are common among learners of English.

LEAD-IN

01 Start by telling students what you had for breakfast or lunch and asking them what they had. Draw 2 columns on the board with the headings 'Countable' and 'Uncountable'. Put a food that has been mentioned by you or them into the right column, e.g. chips (countable), rice (uncountable). Ask students to do the exercise in pairs. Have students come up to the board to write the words in the correct column.

1 curry, rice	2 cereal	3 mashed potato
4 fish, chips	5 noodles, vegetables, chicken	
6 chicken, salad	7 toast	8 burger
Countable:	burger, chip, noodle, vegetable	
Uncountable:	cereal, chicken, curry, fish, mashed potato, rice, salad, toast	

02 In small groups, students discuss the questions about food. When they mention different foods, ask them to add them to the lists on the board.

03 Ask students to read the title of the text. Elicit or explain meaning of 'culture shock' (feelings of confusion when experiencing a culture which is very different to one's own for the first time). Tell students that people are often 'shocked' by other cultures' eating habits. Ask students to look at the pictures as a clue to the content of the text.

It is important to keep to the time limit of one minute in order to encourage skim reading.

Advice

Give time limits to activities as they help students understand how much detail they need to go into, or in this case, which reading style to adopt. Giving them a chance to speak briefly about anything they remember gives them an initial reason for reading as well as extra speaking practice.

04 Try to elicit from students how they should approach this exercise. (Highlight key words in questions, think of synonyms for them, scan the text for the key words/synonyms, read the relevant part in detail).

Alternative

Do exercise 04 as a race between individuals, pairs or groups.

1 daal	2 chicken	3 China
4 burgers	5 India	6 burgers

05 Exercise 05 provides examples of how questions are often paraphrases of parts of the text. Rather than just focusing on the answers to the task, students need to concentrate on finding the evidence, which consists of a paraphrase of the question.

Sometimes paraphrase involves interpretation of an example- students need to work out what it is an example of. E.g. 'grow their own vegetables' and 'keep chickens' are examples of 'producing your own food'. Other times, it is just a case of identifying synonyms, e.g. 'illogical' and 'random'.

After students match questions and evidence, they find the answers to the questions.

1 f	2 d	3 a	4 e	5 b	6 c

06 Remind students of the need to read instructions carefully to see how many words are needed and where the words come from: the box or the text.

Before getting students to do exercise 6, ask them what part of speech is the word they are looking for in each sentence, e.g. in question 1, a noun and in question 2 a verb.

Alternative

If your class is stronger, you could ask them to predict which words go in the gaps. Were any of their predictions correct?

1 repeate	2 identity	3 palm(s)	4 prosperity
5 Asia			

GRAMMAR FOCUS: COUNTABLE AND UNCOUNTABLE NOUNS

07 This exercise focuses on common errors that students make in this area, including the singular/plural verb forms and use of articles.

Remind students that uncountable and singular nouns take a singular verb form such as 'is' and countable nouns which are plural take a plural form such as 'are'.

1. Fresh fruit **is** healthy and we should eat **it** everyday.
2. Chips cooked in the oven **are** healthier than fried chips.
3. Burgers and pizza are the cheapest foods you can buy.
4. In India it is easy to find vegetarian food.
5. My favourite food is chicken.

Advice

Whenever students do written work, use their errors to construct exercises for the class. Choose errors that several students have made and copy them to create an error correction worksheet. You should not reveal who made the mistakes to avoid embarrassing students.

08 Point out to students that 'much' tends to be used in questions and negatives rather than positive statements.

He eats much rice X

He eats a lot of rice. (tick)

1 some	2 many	3 much
4 any/much	5 some	6 much

EXAM SKILLS

The reading passage contains information about famous chefs the students probably haven't heard of. However, this is likely to be the case in the exam so they should get used to using the passage to do the task and not worrying about anything they have not heard of.

09 This activity will require students to recognise synonyms and paraphrase.

1 F	2 B	3 A	4 E	5 G	6 F	7 D

10 Point out to students that this exercise will need them to scan the text for the chefs' names.

1 C	2 E	3 B	4 A	5 F	6 D	7 E

WRITING

OUTCOMES

- deal with a Part 1 question with two diagrams
- describe data without exact numbers
- compare data in a pie chart
- decide what information to include.

OUTCOMES

This lesson gives students practice in tasks with two different but related diagrams. For Task 1, students need to be able to use a variety of expressions to describe data without using the actual numbers, for example fractions or saying whether the proportion of something is high or low. The language of comparison is often needed in Task 1. Students will not do well in Task 1 if they are not able to select the most important information. Both describing everything or selecting less important information will limit their scores.

LEAD-IN

01 Give students a minute or two to look at the diagrams on their own. Ask a few general questions about the data, such as

a) What happened to the number of Indian restaurants between 1960 and 2015?

b) How many categories are there in the pie chart?

c) What is the most popular type of takeaway?

d) Then ask students how the two diagrams are related.

02 This exercise aims to raise awareness of the fact that there are certain phrases/language associated with certain types of data.

Extension

Can students think of other phrases that could be used with these charts?

Diagram 1: 1, 2, 5, 6
Diagram 2: 3, 4, 7

03 Start with the tip. When there are two diagrams, students need to carefully study how they are connected. This is another opportunity to clarify the difference between an introduction and an overview. Students should be able to complete the gaps easily by studying the diagrams. Ask:

Does the introductory sentence include both diagrams? (Yes)Does the overview include both diagrams? (Yes)

Remind students that the overview actually gives some key data, while the introduction tells us what kind of data it is.

1 pie	2 bar	3 1960
4 2015	5 Chinese	6 increased/rose/grew

04 Using this kind of expression shows the examiner that the student has understood the data and also widens the range of vocabulary and sentence structure used.

1 c 34% - just over a third
2 b 26% - about a quater
3 d 10% - one in ten
4 a 1% - a tiny proportion

Extension

If you have a stronger class, you could introduce some more fractions (e.g. two thirds, a fifth, three quarters, etc.)

GRAMMAR FOCUS: COUNTABLE AND UNCOUNTABLE NOUNS

05-09 The grammar section in this lesson links comparison to countable/uncountable nouns in that 'less' is used with uncountable nouns while 'fewer' is used with countable nouns.

For exercise 05 you might need to give a few examples before students do the exercise, depending on your class. Once they have the correct answers to exercise 05, they will be able to work out the rule in exercise 06.

Do exercise 07 on the board. If students ask about other words, or if they need more support, you can add additional words to the list.

Extension

If students are interested, they could extend this comparison between the two countries or compare other countries they know about for further practice.

05

| 1 most | 2 least | 3 more |
| 4 less | 5 More | 6 Fewer |

06

| 1 uncountable | 2 countable |

07

Countable: animal, country, farm, home, language, person, restaurant
Uncountable: coffee, land*, meat, oil, sand
* When land means 'country', it is countable.

08

| 1 more | 2 less | 3 fewer | 4 more |

GRAMMAR FOCUS: ARTICLES

09

1 **The** number of Indian restaurants in **the** UK has risen.
2 Chinese food is the most popular.
3 **The** second most popular food is Indian.
4 There was **a** small drop in the number of Indian restaurants in 2011.
5 There were about **a** thousand Indian restaurants in 1970.

Exercise 09 focuses on common errors with articles. These include both including articles where they are not needed (the Chinese food) and missing out articles. Remind students that a singular, countable noun follows a determiner (usually but not always an article). For example 'There was small drop…'. 'Drop' is a singular, countable noun, so the indefinite article 'a' is needed before it. In this case, the article goes before the adjective 'small'.

10 This exercise also encourages students to use a range of expressions. It is also more accurate to use this type of expression because only tasks with the data displayed in a table will have exact figures.

Extension

Give students some more numbers and ask them to describe them without giving the exact number.

| 1 c | 2 f | 3 e | 4 a | 5 b | 6 d |

11 Ask students to read the sentences and then look at the diagram about supermarkets. Before looking at sentences 01 to 05, students make some general comments about the data.

Ask students for the exact figures, e.g. What was the market share of Alton in 1995? They will probably give different answers (10,10.5,11). This is why it is often necessary to avoid giving exact figures.

Alternative

Ask students some general questions about the data before they complete the gapped sentences, e.g.

Which supermarket had the biggest market share in 2015?

Which is the least popular of the four supermarkets?

| 1 just under /a little under; just over /a little over |
| 2 just under / a little under |
| 3 between |
| 4 approximately/around/about |
| 5 approximately/around/about |

12 Start with the tip. Task 1 tests students' ability to describe the data given. The unnecessary sentences represent the student's opinion on the data: 'It is not surprising…' and some information from outside the data: 'Even my village has an Indian restaurant!' Opinions can be given in task 2 not task 1.

The sentences that should not be included are:
It is not surprising that people in the UK like British food as fish and chips is the national dish.
Even my village has an Indian restaurant!

13 This exercise shows students how the various exercises they have done link to an actual exam task. Get students to study model answers carefully, picking out examples of these aspects.

1 We can see that Chinese and Indian takeaways are the favourites, and that the number of Indian restaurants in the UK rose steadily during this period.
2 The pie chart shows us that Indian food is popular and the bar chart shows how its popularity has grown. The introductory sentence [*The pie chart shows which type of takeaway food is the most popular in the UK, while the bar chart shows how many Indian restaurants existed in the UK between 1960 and 2015.*] also mentions the two charts, though it doesn't interpret the information to make a clear link between them.
3 Chinese and Indian takeaways are much more popular than all the others
4 were only chosen by 1% of people
5 in the 1990s
6 has remained stable
7 from about 5000 … to almost 8000

EXAM SKILLS

14 Check that students understand the difference between 'overweight' and 'obese'. Obese is a medical term to describe a Body Mass Index (BMI) of over 30. Severely obese is a BMI above 40.

The questions are to help guide students through the task and locate the most relevant information to use in their report.

1 The percentage of overweight or obese adults is increasing.

2 the period between 1985 and 1995

3 There was a similar, slightly larger increase.

4 The pie chart looks at the number of overweight and obese people in a single year and gives information about how obese they are.

5 6%

6 The largest group is people who are obese, but apart from the severely obese group, the groups are very similar in size.

15 The amount of support given here will depend on your class. You could guide them through the questions or just let them do the task individually either as a timed essay in class or for homework.

Sample answer

The bar chart shows the percentage of the adult population who were overweight or obese between 1965 and 2015, while the pie chart shows the percentage of people who were a healthy weight, overweight, obese and extremely obese in 2015. The rise in the number of people who are too heavy was gradual from 1965 to 1985. The first significant increase occurred between 1985 and 1995, from around 48% to almost 60%. In the next ten-year period there was a similar large rise. By 2005, approximately 70% of people weighed too much. The upward trend continued into the 21st century but at a slightly lower rate.

The pie chart confirms that in 2015 over 70% of adults were too heavy, and it also gives more detail about how much they were overweight. Only 6.3% of people were so overweight that their health was seriously at risk, i.e. severely obese. The remaining people were divided more or less equally between the other groups.

Feedback

Acknowledge students' attempts to describe the data, using relevant expressions covered in the unit, such as 'about a third'. Give extra marks for introductory sentences and overviews, which include both diagrams.

LISTENING

OUTCOMES

- find synonyms and paraphrase in matching tasks
- identify 'distractors' in matching tasks
- answer classification tasks.

OUTCOMES

This lesson helps students to identify distractors in listening tasks. There are a few techniques, which are often used so students will be able to listen out for them and avoid the wrong answers. It also gives them practice at the kind of task where they have to group items into categories or 'classification' and matching tasks'.

Distractor

This is a wrong answer in a task, which involves selecting from a list of possible answers. They are designed to 'distract' students from the correct answer.

LEAD-IN

01 Students match the pictures to the verbs.

Ask students what kind of food is prepared using these methods.

Extension

For stronger classes you could elicit some other cooking methods.

A boil	B fry	C bake	D grill

02 After doing the exercise, you could get students to add a few more foods to each category.

Alternative

Depending on your class, you might want to focus on the pronunciation of these words, including sounds and word stress. For example, you could get student to mark the stressed syllables or point out that 'cake' rhymes with 'steak' but 'peas' doesn't rhyme with 'pears'.

Extension

Ask students which foods they like or dislike and how they would cook them.

MEAT DISHES: lamb, beef, steak, burger
VEGETABLES: potatoes, cucumbers, carrots, peas
FRUITS: apples, strawberries, pears, bananas
SWEETS: cake, chocolate, pastries, biscuits

03 This task represents a typical way of introducing distractors. One speaker makes a suggestion and the other either accepts or rejects it. Students can be easily distracted if they don't recognise the pattern and stop listening. For example, when a student hears: 'We could have pizza. Everybody likes pizza', he or she could think they have heard the correct answer. Stress that students need to keep listening to see if that was a distractor, which in this case it was.

Transcript 32

Mike:	So, what type of meal do you think we should have at the party, Jane?
Jane:	I don't know, Mike. Do you have any ideas?
Mike:	What do you think about preparing a Mexican meal?
Jane:	I really like Mexican food and we could have some fun Mexican party games, but I think that it might be too spicy for some people.
Mike:	That's true. … We could have pizza? Everybody likes pizza.

Jane:	Hmm, I think we should have something healthier.
Mike:	I know! We could have salad and roast chicken.
Jane:	That sounds like a good idea. And it's fairly simple to prepare. Let's do that.

> 1 c   2 a   3 b
> They are going to prepare salad and roast chicken.

04 This is a similar example but in this case, the speakers reject the correct answer (boil) once, reject the others and come back to boil. It is important that students are aware of these techniques. In this case, having heard all the options rejected, they may panic and think there is no correct answer. It is important to listen carefully and be patient.

Transcript 33

A:	So do you think that we now have everything ready for the meal?
B:	Almost, I was just wondering what would be the best way of preparing the potatoes.
A:	Well, you could just boil them and serve them with the fish.
B:	That would be easy, but I don't think it would be very exciting.
A:	What about frying them? Everybody likes fried potatoes.
B:	They aren't very healthy though, and I haven't got much oil left.
A:	You could bake them and serve them with the salad Nina's preparing.
B:	That would taste good, but it takes ages to bake potatoes in the oven. I know, I'll boil them and then put them with Nina's salad.

> A is the correct answer. Frying the potatoes won't be healthy, baking the potatoes will take too long.

05 Refer students to the tip and tell them that there may be more options than are needed.

This exercise demonstrates clearly that there is usually a lot of irrelevant information, which students need to ignore. Although 'cakes and pastries' (sweets) are mentioned, the shop they will be bought from is not given.

Another distraction is that they talk about 'cucumbers' (a vegetable) while talking about Arcadia, but the speaker didn't actually buy them from there.

Extension

You could refer students to the audio-script and get them to highlight the part of the dialogue that they actually need to answer the questions.

Transcript 34

A:	Before we go back to the flat, I think we need to check we have everything that we need.
B:	OK, well you went to Arcadia, so I imagine that you got the strawberries and apples from there?
A:	Yes, I did.
B:	Did you notice if they had any cucumbers while you were over there?
A:	I'm not sure, I thought *you* were going to get them.
B:	Well I went over to Best Buy, and I got some nice carrots and peas, but I didn't like the look of the cucumbers.
A:	Oh, I suppose we can go there on the way back to the station.
B:	Don't forget we need to get some cakes and pastries too. We can get those after we've been to Hampton's to get the lamb and chicken.
A:	OK, good plan.

> 1 C   2 A   3 B
> Option D was mentioned, but it didn't match any of the shops.

06 In this exercise, there are more distractors than in the previous one. Point out that the restaurant types that are not needed are mentioned in the dialogues. In some cases, two distractors are introduced together: Is it a French restaurant or a steakhouse?

Paraphrase is important here. The answer to question 1 (Adam's) is given as 'It serves food from all over the world', which is a paraphrase of 'international'.

Transcript 35

A:	In this new series of 'Talk of the Town' we'll be looking at the different restaurants in and around Ogdenville and getting some tips and recommendations from our resident food critic, Chris Griffin. So Chris, where have you been this week?
B:	Well, one restaurant that I really enjoyed is Adam's. It's on the Town Square. I ordered a steak au poivre and it was perfect.
A:	What's that?
B:	It's a steak in peppercorns – it's quite a typical French dish.
A:	So, is it a French restaurant or a steakhouse?
B:	Well, the chef is French, but it serves food from all over the world. It has a wide variety of dishes. One word of warning though, it gets really busy at weekends, so you should check they have places before you go.

A: Have you got any other recommendations for us this week, Chris?

B: Oh, yes. I can really recommend the Duke on Smith Street. I had lobster and it was really tasty. It also has a few vegetarian dishes, but it's the fish dishes that make it famous in the town. The food isn't that low-cost though, so you might want to save going here for a special treat.

A: What about people who are on a budget? Have you got any suggestions for them?

B: Yes, I have. The Tower in Market Street is a fashionable restaurant where people can get a good meal at a reasonable price. I had a pizza, but it isn't a fast food restaurant, it specialises in all different types of food from Italy. I've heard that the lasagne is especially good.

A: Thanks, Chris. You certainly have given us all food for thought.

1 E	2 C	3 D

07 It is useful for students to carefully study the audio-script to understand how distractors work in the Listening texts. Ask them to highlight the right answers and distractors in different colours.

> 1 The interviewer asks if Adam's is a French restaurant (F) or a steakhouse (B), but Chris says it *sells food from all over the world*, so E is the correct answer.
>
> 2 Vegetarian (A) dishes are mentioned when Chris talks about The Duke, but *it's the fish dishes make it famous* and so it can't be a vegetarian restaurant.
>
> 3 Chris says that The Tower isn't a fast food restaurant (G) and *it specialises in all different types of food from Italy* so D is the correct answer

Advice

Allow students to listen with the audio-script after they have listened at least once without it.

08 Studying the audio-script after listening also gives students the chance to study language and build their vocabulary, including synonyms.

1 busy	2 tasty	3 low-cost
4 fashionable	5 reasonable	

09-10 Students will probably find a lot of new language in this exercise. It is often the 'new' word, which is the one that helped them find the answer. Let students spend time on this exercise, looking up and noting down the new words and their synonyms.

Do question 1 as an example. Write the sentence 'The price of food in the restaurant is not cheap.' on the board. Elicit synonyms and antonyms for 'cheap'. Elicit different ways of expressing the idea. Ask students to read the three paraphrases and decide which one does not have the same meaning.

09

1 C	2 B	3 A	4 C	5 A	6 C	7 C	8 B

10

1 cheap – reasonable, budget
2 tasty – delicious, mouth-watering
3 old-fashioned – traditional, historic
4 street – outdoors, from stalls in the streets
5 skilful – expertise, highly trained
6 can be changed – use different ingredients, flexible
7 famous – well known, recognized
8 too spicy – too much pepper, too hot

11 Inform students that the sentences 1 to 5 are paraphrases rather than the actual words from the audio.

This exercise also lends itself well to a detailed study of the audio-script, looking for examples of paraphrase. However, this will be most useful to a class that has difficulty with the exercise.

Tell students they must always take their answers from the listening text and not from their own knowledge. Even if the topic is one they are familiar with (and even if they disagree with the information given), they must answer according to the text.

Transcript 36

Chef: I suppose one thing that everybody knows about Japanese, Chinese and Korean cooking is that they all use chopsticks rather than knives and forks like people in the West. The chopsticks that people use in the different countries are quite different though. In China the chopsticks tend to be made of wood and are round at the end, whereas in Korea they're made of stainless steel and are rough at the end. This is because in the past the emperor would use silver chopsticks, as they changed colour if there was any poison in the dish. They can be quite tricky to use, but in Korea people use a spoon to eat their rice. In Japan they use a variety of things to make chopsticks. Wood and plastic are the most popular now, but you can find bone, metal and even ivory ones.

If we look at the food of the different countries, it's very difficult to talk about China in general terms because it has many different cuisines. So it might be better if we look at Korean and Japanese food a little more. It's well known that Koreans tend to like spicier food and red peppers can be found in a wide number of dishes. I suppose that everybody thinks of sushi when they think of Japanese food, but you can also find a lot of influences from all over Asia and even Europe, for example tempura, which came to Japan from Portugal. Those aren't present in Chinese and Korean food.

Traditionally, in both Japan and in Korea meat plays less of an important role than in Europe, perhaps because it's so expensive due to the lack of space for keeping animals. That said, both the Japanese and Koreans enjoy meat. Barbecues of all types are popular in Korea and beef forms the basis of many special meals in both of the countries. Now moving back to Chinese cuisine …

| 1 B | 2 A | 3 C | 4 B | 5 C |

EXAM SKILLS

12 The exam skills questions gives students more practice at the type of task where there are more answers than questions. Again, all the types of food are mentioned in the text but they don't all relate to one of the four questions, so students will need to listen carefully.

Transcript 37

Interviewer: Today in the studio I am pleased to have with me the famous chef, Graham Shepherd. Graham has just come back from Beijing in China, where he was making a TV programme on the food that you can try in this historic city. So, Graham, what can you tell us about your trip? Was it how you expected it to be?

Graham: It was quite surprising really. I suppose that most people think of Beijing duck when they think of Beijing and I did try some of this tasty traditional dish, but with so many people from all over the country living in Beijing there really are a lot of different foods from all regions of the country. One dish that I really enjoyed and I didn't expect to find was kebabs. These tasty snacks are originally from North West China, but they're very popular street food in Beijing. They're especially popular as a tasty snack at lunchtime for school pupils. They have less meat and more vegetables than *we* are used to, so they're a bit healthier.

Interviewer: I'm sure that most people have tried kebabs, but did you try anything that might be unusual for our listeners?

Graham: Oh, yes. One of the things that I had was jellyfish. It added a nice texture to the dish, but I thought it didn't taste of much. One dish that did have a strong taste was hotpot. The dish I had was made in the Sichuan style, so it was very spicy. What I found interesting was that the hotpot was put on a hotplate in the centre of the table, and we were given a dish of raw food and we chose what we wanted and put it into the pot ourselves, and got it out when it was ready. It was great fun and very sociable. And very tasty!

Interviewer: I'm sure that you tried some of the dishes that we all know and love too. Can you tell us something interesting about them?

Graham: Of course, everybody knows about noodles and dumplings, but I doubt many people know how many different types there are! One of the highlights for me was learning how to make fresh noodles with a chef from Northern China. The recipe of egg, salt and wheat flour is quite simple, but to make the noodles by hand you need to be quite a skilful chef.

Something which is much simpler to make are dumplings. The basic ingredients are flour and water, but the beauty of this dish is that it's very flexible. You can fill them with whatever you like. I especially enjoyed one with raw prawns, but all sorts of meat and vegetables can be put in them.

Interviewer: Thanks Graham, that's really interesting, but unfortunately we've run out of time. If you'd like to know more about Graham's adventures, the series will be starting on Thursday at 7 o'clock on Channel 9.

| 1 B | 2 E | 3 D | 4 C |

SPEAKING

OUTCOMES

- talk about food in your country (Speaking Part 1)
- use the preparation time to collect your ideas for Part 2
- organise your talk (Speaking Part 2).

OUTCOMES

Food and the habits around eating in the student's country are popular topics in the speaking test. In this lesson, students broaden their food vocabulary and practise preparing for task 2.

LEAD-IN

01 Students might not be familiar with all these dishes. Stress that it doesn't matter if they get the right answers. It is an introduction to describing a dish and some common ingredients. Check meaning of the word 'ingredients' and also the ingredients themselves.

Suggested answers
1 **Arabian Kabsa:** chicken, onions, garlic, tomatoes, spices, carrots
2 **Pizza:** flour, cheese, tomatoes (and other toppings)
3 **Egg noodles and Chinese dumplings:** egg, flour, beef, onions, cabbage

02 Students could also use some of the cooking methods from the Listening lesson (e.g. boil, fry, etc.), if appropriate

Alternative

Students describe a dish and its ingredients and their partner has to guess what it is.

GRAMMAR FOCUS: COUNTABLE AND UNCOUNTABLE NOUNS

03

1 are a lot of	2 isn't much	3 is a lot of
4 are some	5 aren't any	6 is some

Transcript 38

Examiner: What kind of food is popular in your country?

Mohammed: These days a lot of young people actually enjoy Western food like pizza and fried chicken. Our national food is often too spicy, especially for children and foreigners, and also it takes too long to cook. I think that it's delicious though!

Examiner: What do you think of Western food?

Mohammed: Well, I suppose Western food is quick to make and is tasty too, so everyone can eat it without too much trouble. I think that a lot of people like food to be convenient because they're so busy nowadays.

Examiner: Is there any kind of food you don't like?

Mohammed: Yes, I'm not keen on sushi at all. It's so strange eating something that hasn't been cooked. I know it's very fresh and healthy but I just don't like the taste and I can't stand the texture – it's too chewy for me.

04 This exercise demonstrates the length of ideal answers to Part 1 questions. Point out that the student uses a range of language to give his opinions on food. Students often think 'too' is the same as 'very'. By putting the expressions with 'too' into the 'negative' column, they should realise too +adjective is negative, even if the adjective is generally positive, e.g. 'too sweet'.

Positive: enjoy, delicious, quick to make, is tasty, convenient, fresh, healthy

Negative: too spicy, takes too long to cook, not keen on, so strange, don't like the taste, can't stand, too chewy

05 If appropriate, pair students with someone they don't usually work with. Encourage them to use 'too+ adjective' with other adjectives as well as the phrases Mohammed used.

Circulate and correct students where necessary.

Point out common errors, if any, at the end, by writing them on the board as well as the correct forms.

06 This activity demonstrates how to use the task card as a plan. Although the speaker covers all the points in the task, her talk flows naturally between points. Ask students to study and label the audio-script to help them understand the relationship between the task card and the talk.

Transcript 39

Angelica: I'm going to talk about an Italian dish – risotto. It's a rice dish and most people in my country enjoy it. Unlike in most countries, we fry the rice with onion in olive oil before we add any liquid. We don't cook it in water, but a kind of soup or broth, which can be made of meat, fish or chicken. I'm from Milan, and our traditional risotto is made using saffron, which gives the dish a beautiful yellow colour. It's a very creamy and delicious dish. We usually have it as a starter, not as the main meal.

Firstly, I think that it's popular in my country because – and not a lot of people know this – but Italy's one of the biggest producers of rice in Europe. It's very simple to cook, and as I said before, you can use all types of ingredients. Anything that you can find in the fridge! Also, Italians don't like to waste food, so if you have some fish or some meat and it isn't enough for a meal, you can always make risotto.

I love it first of all because it always reminds me of home. My mother's very fond of cooking risotto and if I was unhappy, she used to make it for me and it always cheered me up. I don't live at home now and so when I'm feeling homesick and missing my family, I always try to find an Italian restaurant and have some risotto! And secondly, I like it because it's a great meal to make for friends – easy to prepare, but very tasty.

You can get risotto everywhere nowadays, but it isn't always that good. If you visit my country, especially the northern part, I recommend that you try to taste risotto there. It really is special and I promise that you will find it different to any risotto that you have tasted before.

1 Yes

2 risotto

3 a lot of rice is produced there, simple to cook, you can use different ingredients

4 It reminds him of home. It's a good meal to make for friends.

5 Because it is special and tastes different to risotto in other countries.

07 This exercise shows how a student has addressed every point on the task card in his/her notes.

Point out some of the words and phrases which students may find useful when doing this task: traditional, proud of, street food, tasty, reminds me of, grilled, serve with

1 d	2 a	3 c	4 b

08 Time students and see if they can write notes in one minute. They may need more practice as one minute gives them very little thinking time.

Alternative

Let students take a bit longer to prepare their note cards at this stage.

09 Consider pairing up stronger and weaker students here. This will mean the stronger one will be able to think of questions to ask the weaker one if he/she stops talking too soon. Time students.

Weaker students can aim for one minute while stronger ones aim for two. In practice, any length between one and two minutes is acceptable. The advantage of using the whole two minutes is they can demonstrate they know more language.

10 Students should aim to build up a list of phrases that can help them signpost their talk. This exercise provides a useful starting point.

1 I	2 I	3 C	4 C	5 C

11 Ask students to work with a different partner, if appropriate. Give them time to study the notes and ask for clarification. They take it in turns (one is Student A, the other is Student B) to talk from the notes.

Extension

Ask students to give each other feedback on their talks. For example, did they miss anything out? Did they hesitate for too long? Were there any grammatical or pronunciation errors?

EXAM SKILLS

12 Refer students to the tip. Write 'Good' and 'Bad' on the board as column headers. Tell students you are looking at different ways to describe food. Ask students to come and add words to the lists. Remind them of any that have come up in any lesson of this unit. Tell students to try and use a variety of the words in their talk.

Check meaning of 'occasion' and elicit examples they could talk about (birthday party, wedding, festival, graduation, etc.). Point out that to keep talking for 2 minutes, they will need to add quite a few details, so for 'what you ate', they can explain the dish, ingredients, preparation methods. Elicit possible answers for 'who was at the meal' (colleagues, neighbours, relations, etc.) Elicit reasons why a meal could be enjoyable (the food, atmosphere, meeting old friends, etc.)

Feedback

Peers will be one source of feedback as you won't be able to listen to everyone.

Ask partners to make sure the speaker included all the main points and spoke for 1-2 minutes without hesitation.

You could ask for a few students to volunteer to give their talk to the class and give feedback on content, organisation, delivery and language.

Advice

Over the course, try to listen to different students talking at length so they all receive individual feedback from you. You should also guide students towards giving useful feedback to their peers.

UNIT / 05: CONSUMERISM

READING

OUTCOMES

- identify topic sentences
- identify main and supporting ideas
- match headings with paragraphs
- use *will* and *going to*.

OUTCOMES

In IELTS reading it is important for students to be able to identify the main idea of a paragraph, expressed in a 'topic sentence'.

Topic sentence

This is the sentence in each paragraph that introduces the main idea of the paragraph. The other sentences in the paragraph support and give examples of this main idea.

In this way they will be able to skim above supporting details when time is limited. It also makes it easier for them to match headings with paragraphs since the headings will be based on the main idea.

The unit also introduces two future forms, will and going to. Although there are several other ways to talk about the future, these two are common and a useful introduction to talking about the future.

LEAD-IN

01 Check students know the meaning of a mall. Mention a local one to illustrate.

All of the activities mentioned are possible at malls somewhere in the world though some are probably not in the students' local mall.

Extension

Ask students to discuss in groups:

What have you done at the mall recently?

Do you like going to malls?

What do you like about your local mall?

According to the text, all these activities can be done at a mall.

The pictures show bungee jumping, a beauty treatment, skiing, a health check and having an expensive meal.

02 Give students one minute to read, reminding them to move their eyes across and down very quickly. When the time is up, see if they noticed any of the activities in exercise 1. Don't tell them the answers but give them another two minutes to see if they can complete their answers to the 3 questions.

1 All of the activities are mentioned.

2 The text mentions the US, New China the Middle East, East Asia, Bangkok, Singapore, Madrid, London.

3 It is about the present and future.

03 The technique of 'sampling' a text is based on the idea that the topic sentence tends to be the first one. As we see in this text, in the first paragraph it is not. Sampling involves reading the whole of the first and last paragraphs because these are the paragraphs most likely to have the topic sentence in a different place

Sampling a text

Reading the first and last paragraphs and the first sentence of each paragraph in between. This has the same aim as skimming.

In Paragraph B, the topic sentence is the first one. Students locate the supporting evidence in the paragraph.

(1) Asia and not the US is now the 'mall capital' of the world and is home to the five largest malls in the world. (2) China is home to the two largest.

04-05 In these exercises, the students study the paragraphs carefully, identifying topic sentences and supporting evidence. Students at this level will find it difficult to paraphrase so just substituting different words is a good way to start. Depending on your class, they might need support with writing the ideas in their own words. They should, however, be starting to identify paraphrase. Read through the box on paraphrase carefully with them.

04

C Malls are becoming 'the new downtown', with cinemas, bowling alleys and even concert halls.

D Mall owners are going to need to think of new ideas to remain in business.

E Malls will need to consider the environment too.

05 *Possible answers*

C There will be more fine dining / there will be spas, fitness centres and art galleries / there will be more apartments and office space.

D There are 'pop-up' shops, stall and kiosks at different times of the year.

E Malls will have to make sure people can reach them by public transport / Malls will have to use natural sources of heat and light / There will be more plants, trees, grass and waterfalls.

06-08 These exercises are closely linked. They introduce the idea that the headings may be paraphrases or include synonyms from the main idea in the paragraph. Allow the students to use dictionaries if necessary. Carefully studying the language in exercise 07, should hopefully allow them to find the correct answers in exercise 08.

07

1 c	2 e	3 a	4 f	5 b	6 d

08

B iii	C v	D i	E iv

GRAMMAR FOCUS: FUTURE FORMS

09 Ask students to focus on the text so they don't spot the answers, 'will' and 'going to' in the box.

Students probably already use 'will' and 'going to' in their own speech, but they are unlikely to be aware of the difference between them. Students tend to think of 'will' as 'the future' and overuse it, so these exercises should raise awareness of the difference.

You could illustrate the use of 'going to' using your immediate surroundings. If there are grey clouds in the sky, you could point at them and say 'It's going to rain'. You could also talk about your plans, e.g. 'I'm going to give you homework today' and show them the handouts you have already prepared.

Elicit examples of 'will' and 'going to' from the text:

will – So what **will** the mall of the future **look** like? / It is predicted that this **will happen** more and more in the future. / Some malls **will** only **sell** electrical items / Some malls **will** only **include** expensive shops / the facilities malls **will need to** offer / Malls **will need to** consider the environment too. / There **will be** more open-air malls / designers **will have to** make sure / They **will also need to** use more natural sources of heat and light / We **will see** more plants, trees / there will be 'virtual malls' / technology will be used within malls / the mall will go from strength to strength
going to – in the future we are going to see 'fine dining' too / There **are also going to be** more apartments / Mall owners **are going to need to** think of new ideas

10 Before they start the exercise, remind students that there should be some evidence of a plan or a start to the change for 'going to' to be used. Get students to check their answers together before checking as a class.

Extension

Ask students to make their own sentences with 'will' and 'going to'.

1 is going to	2 are going to	3 will
4 will / are going to	5 are going to	6 will

EXAM SKILLS

11-12 The amount of support you give students will depend on your class. If they are struggling, you can exploit the pictures and have a discussion about markets to get thinking about the topic of the text, for example:

Ask students to look at the pictures on the pages and name the items they can see. Provide any words they don't know.

Ask them about markets they have visited. What did they buy there? Can they buy different things at different types of the year? (Pre-teach 'seasonal' markets).

If your class is ready for it, give them the exercises as exam practice in or out of class.

11

1 F	2 D	3 B	4 C	5 E

12

1 B ii	2 C iv	3 D vii	4 E i	5 F vi

WRITING

OUTCOMES

- organise a Part 2 essay
- write an introduction
- write about points for and against, and give opinions
- give examples and evidence to support your views.

OUTCOMES

In this lesson we move on to writing Part 2. Students will learn some language for giving their opinions and presenting the pros and cons of an issue. They will need to provide evidence to back up their main points and to structure an essay properly.

LEAD-IN

01 Tell students, that in Part 2 essays they should present both sides of an argument and give an opinion. Give students time to fill in the table. Help them with the pronunciation of new words.

Extension

Can students brainstorm and add any more expressions?

Good points: advantages, benefits, positive aspects
Bad points: disadvantages, drawbacks, negative aspects
Opinion: all things considered, in my view, personally

02 Check the meaning of 'shopping' online before having students do the exercise either alone or in pairs.

Alternative

If you have a strong class who have lots of ideas, you could start by eliciting the advantages and disadvantages of shopping online as well as their own opinions. They could then do the exercise and see if their ideas were mentioned.

2 B	3 O	4 G	5 G	6 B	7 O	8 B	9 O

03 Ask students how they find out about the news. What newspapers and websites do they read (in their first language too)? Draw their attention to the tip and emphasise that they need to know what is going on around the world so that they will have ideas and examples for their essay.

Even if the essay asks students to agree or disagree it is better to give at least one reason why some people have the opposite view.

1 c	2 a	3 b

04 Many young students find deciding on their own opinion (and coming up with reasons) one of the hardest parts of the IELTS writing paper. This exercise gives them four points of view to choose from.

Read out the tip. Emphasise that the essay doesn't have to be based on students' actual opinions. They should choose a stance they can find supporting evidence for. They must not say 'I haven't decided about this issue yet' or 'I have never thought about this before'!

Alternative

Students work in four groups according to their opinion, A, B, C or D. In those groups they come up with additional reasons for their choice.

05 Sometimes a question students have practised will come up in the exam in a slightly different way. They need to read the question carefully and adapt the ideas from the previous essay so that they answer the question set.

Suggested answers
Advantages: 1, 2, 5, 7
Disadvantages: 3, 4, 6, 8

06 In Part 2 students should write a full introduction with about 3 or 4 sentences (an introductory paragraph). This contrasts with Part 1 in which they only have to write an introductory sentence.

Different essay types will differ slightly in terms of what is included in the introduction, as some require the student's opinion. However, all introductions should have a general comment on the current situation.

Introduction B is better because the writer's opinion is not given the introduction. In an 'advantages/disadvantages' essay it is better to give views on both sides before you give your own opinion. Introduction A also gives some of the main points in favour of supermarkets, which is not appropriate in an introduction.

07 Students work in pairs or small groups to evaluate this introduction. Remind them to refer to the instruction box to do this.

See exercise 08.

08 Refer students back to the question. A good point of the essay is that the student has not revealed his or her own opinion. In this kind of essay, students should look at both sides, weigh the evidence and give their own view at the end.

09 Ask students some questions to elicit the current situation with regards to a 'cashless society'.

How often do you/your parents use credit/debit cards?

Do you/your parents pay bills online?

What do you/they still pay for by cash?

Refer them to the picture of a 'contactless' payment? Do they use them yet?

Establish that generally society is moving away from cash, although most are not completely 'cashless' yet.

Ask them if they should give their opinion in the introduction. (No, in an advantages/disadvantages essay it will come at the end).

Remind them that they should state their intentions (plan) in the introduction.

Feedback

Tick each of the valid sentences. Don't focus too much on language errors.

Use peer correction to save time.

Sample introduction

More and more people are relying on debit and credit cards to pay for things in shops and online. If this trend continues, we might become a 'cashless society'. There are both advantages and disadvantages to this, as I will outline in this essay.

10 This exercise aims to raise awareness of the need to support main ideas with specific examples. Check students' understanding of 'specific'.

Extension

Students come up with their own evidence in support of each point. This can be from their own city/country or from something they have read or seen on TV.

1 c	2 d	3 a	4 b

11 Students can work in pairs for this. Remind them to be specific.

Sample answers

1 In my local town the employment offered by the shops is essential as there are not many other jobs.

2 You can get expensive, mid-price and cheap versions of many products.

3 By shopping at the same supermarket you can earn points which save you money.

12 Ask students to brainstorm ideas in groups.

Get students to come to the board to write their ideas so that all the ideas are collected together.

13 Students read the essay and compare with their own ideas.

14 Tell students they are able to complete this plan because it is a well-planned essay. They should aim to construct their essays from a clear plan in the same way.

a goods are all the same

b They have unique items, e.g. antiques.

c Music shops have staff who know about music.

d Small shops give character to a town.

15 This kind of exercise equips students with useful expressions for their own essays. They should organise their notes with a section for linking expressions.

1 my view is, I strongly believe

2 for example, for instance

3 Finally

4 Some people believe that *this is going to happen* …; there *will always be* a place for smaller shops

5 too, however

EXAM SKILLS

16 Ideas for this essay are provided but stronger students might choose not to use them.

Remind students they will have 40 minutes for this essay in the exam but you might want to let them do it in their own time at this stage.

Feedback

When marking this essay, focus on organisation. Have students written a clear introduction? Have they given their opinion in the introduction? Have they looked at both sides of the argument? Check their use of future forms and make sure each idea is clearly supported.

Sample answer

In some countries a mall is known as a shopping centre. The main purpose of a mall was to shop. This is beginning to change and I believe that in the future, the main purpose of a mall will be for entertainment.

More and more of us enjoy shopping online. It is safer than ever and much more convenient. Many websites offer free next-day delivery. On sites like eBay and Amazon, there is far more choice and there are also many discounts and special offers. Obviously, this means that fewer shops will be needed. However, people still want to go out, meet their friends and have fun. A mall is a place which offers space to do that. If people have done their shopping online, the mall will have to offer other facilities to attract visitors.

Some malls already have cinemas and places to eat. However, as well as cheaper cafés and fast food chains, malls are beginning to offer better restaurants and pubs. I believe this trend will continue. In addition, malls will offer all kinds of leisure facilities such as gyms, swimming pools, children's play areas, spas, and so on. There will be more live shows, including music, theatre and dance, and a range of exhibitions and special events.

I believe malls have an important role in future society but they will have a different purpose from today. There will still be a few small shops but most people will go to the mall to relax and enjoy themselves with their family and friends.

LISTENING

OUTCOMES

- answer multiple-choice questions (3 options)
- indentify 'distractors'
- recognise paraphrase and synonyms.

OUTCOMES

This lesson looks at section 2 of the listening test and focuses on answering multiple-choice questions. Refer students back to unit 4 where we looked at some ways in which distractors are presented. Point out that the use of paraphrase and synonyms is a continuing theme because it is so essential in the listening and reading papers.

LEAD-IN

01 Students should be able to do this with ease. Check understanding of 'department store' and give a local example. Shopping centre and mall are the same. Shopping centre is used more in the UK and mall in the US.

A supermarket   B shopping centre
C outdoor market   D department store
E coffee shop

02 After students have completed the listening task, ask them how they decided on the answers. What were the clues that helped them?

Transcript 40

Recording 1

Whatever you do, don't miss our Summer Sale. This weekend and this weekend only, we're reducing all our prices right across our store. So, on our first floor you'll find women's jeans at just twenty dollars a pair. And, just in time for the holiday season, our T-shirts and swimwear are on special offer too. And if you're looking for shoes, you'll want to visit the fourth floor. You'll find a good selection of styles and colours in our footwear department situated right next to coffee shop. This weekend, they're all half price and that includes a wide choice of sports shoes in most sizes! So, hurry before they're all gone! Sale ends Sunday! Miss our sale? Miss out!

Recording 2

Dan: So, Jess, what do you think of my hat?

Jess: It's very nice – I like the colour, and it'll definitely keep the sun off your face. Actually, I didn't notice the clothing stalls.

Dan: I know you didn't! That's because you spent most of your time there looking at all the jewellery! And relaxing in all that fresh air, of course!

Jess: That's true – but actually, I managed to find a really nice necklace. And you'll never guess how cheap it was! Do you want to have a look?

Recording 3

A: So what did you think of it? It only opened a few weeks ago, didn't it?

B: Yes, that's right, so that's why it was very busy. In fact, it was a bit like being at a football match – there were so many people! But I really liked it – it's very convenient because there were at least fifty different shops all under one roof and there's a car park too. I'd really like to go back.

A: Then how about going along there together next weekend? I'd really like to see it for myself. I also need to buy a birthday present for my mum. You could help me choose something for her. And we can go for a coffee afterwards! I'll pay!

1 D	department store	2 C	outdoor market
3 B	shopping centre		

03-04 By reading the questions, students can predict what kind of information will be in the gaps and what kind of information will be in the distractors. For example, there are only a limited number of words that go in the first gap (areas of a town) and the answer to question 2 is clearly something you buy on holiday.

It is useful for students to study the audio-script and identify phrases that are used to introduce both the correct answers (e.g. they have finally decided…) and the distractors (There was talk of…but…)

Transcript 41

Recording 1

And now for the local news … A new branch of Sports World, the Danish sporting goods company, is opening on Saturday. Most of you will be familiar with the branch in the south of Grinstead that opened two years ago and which has enjoyed a lot of success. There was talk of them opening a new store in the Meadows Shopping Centre in the north of the town, but they have finally decided to open in the east, near the football stadium. As a special treat for fans, Grinstead Town's Danish striker Jesper Nielsen will be opening the store ahead of their home match at the weekend.

Recording 2

That is the end of our tour of the city, so you now have a couple of hours to spend some time exploring the city centre. If you want to buy souvenirs, you might find them cheaper near the hotel. However, if you're feeling a bit tired, there are plenty of teashops nearby and they also sell boxes of tea that make really good presents. A word of warning, you'll find a lot of cheap electronic stores offering cameras at really low prices. They might seem good quality, but we've had a lot of complaints from tourists who have bought them, only to find they break after about a week.

Recording 3

Thank you for calling the Eastgate Shopping centre. The centre is currently closed. Our opening days and times are as follows … Monday to Saturday we are open from nine o'clock until six o'clock and on Sunday, our doors open at eleven o'clock and we close at five o'clock.

Recording 4

When I first opened the shop three years ago, we mainly sold shirts and jackets that I had designed, and these proved very popular. However, we added more products as the business started to grow. We also started selling online. The jackets and shirts are still really popular, especially online, but in the shop itself, we sell trousers more than any other item.

03

1 east	2 tea	3 11/eleven	4 trousers

04

5/6 south, north	7/8 souvenirs, cameras
9/10/11 9/nine, 6/six, 5/five	12/13 shirts, jackets

05 This kind of exercise raises awareness of paraphrase and builds students' vocabulary.

Advice

Ask students to make notes of any examples of synonyms/paraphrase they come across. You could ask students to make a wall chart of common synonyms for classroom display.

1 e	2 c	3 d	4 a	5 f	6 b

06 Students should start thinking of possible synonyms and paraphrases for the key words in a question during the preparation time. It would be useful for students to have a copy of the audio-script and highlight where the correct answer comes in each section.

Transcript 42

We also sell a lot of T-shirts. When I first opened the shop, I had a lot of designs that I'd worked on at university and in general these had writing on the front. I thought that it might be fun if people could put a photograph on the T-shirts as well. I invested quite a bit of money in this and they were popular at first. We sometimes have young children who come in with their parents and they buy T-shirts with photographs on. I've stopped designing T-shirts with writing on them, because I don't have the time, so now we sell more T-shirts with nothing on them at all. If fashions change, I might go back to designing them and if you want a photograph on your T-shirt, you know where to come.

A–3   B–2   C–1
Listening: The correct answer is C.

07 It is important to ensure students can recognise different ways of telling the time, e.g. two fifteen/quarter past two. Two thirty/half past two/half two. If they are confused about these, you might want to review expressions of time.

Transcript 43

Calling all fans of Sam West! This famous adventure writer will be in Westfield shopping centre tomorrow in Bookworms Bookshop on the first floor. He will be signing copies of his latest book 'Timed Out'. He is expected to get there at quarter past two and will stay until half past three. Get there as soon as you can because queues will start to form as early as noon. Don't miss this great opportunity to meet everyone's favourite writer!

The key words are 'writer' and 'arrive'.
A noon   B quarter past two   C half past three
Listening: The correct answer is B.

08 Point out to students, that sometimes there is a gap between the key word they will be listening for (in this case, 'complain') and the correct answer. In between, the speaker talks about some things she is happy about (the service and the food) before mentioning the complaint. This will help students be prepared for this pattern.

Transcript 44

I had a great day at that new shopping centre but I would complain about one thing – and not the usual kind of thing – the service in all the shops was good, and I had a delicious lunch in the café on the third floor. No, the annoying thing was the amount of rubbish I saw around me. I think it was because there weren't enough rubbish bins for people to put

their empty cans and sweet wrappers in. But, apart from that, I would say that it's well worth a visit.

Paraphrase A is wrong. The staff are the people who serve the customers.
Listening: The correct answer is B.

EXAM SKILLS

09 Read through the advice box with students. Tell them to use their preparation time to identify key words and possible synonyms.

Remind them that they need to listen to the whole section, which relates to each question before making their decision. The distractors will be mentioned so hearing them doesn't mean they are the right answer.

For homework students can study the audio-script and if they got any wrong, try to understand why.

Have a class discussion about any difficulties encountered. They will find this useful for future listening tasks.

Transcript 45

You will hear a tour guide talking to some tourists. Listen and answer questions 1–6.

Hello everyone. So can you all hear me and see me? OK, my name's David Edwards and I'm your tour leader for your shopping tour today. Now, as you can see, we're parked just in front of the main theatre. If any of you would like tickets for tonight's performance, we can arrange that for you. We're just round the corner from the railway station. If you want to come on our Historic Buildings tour tomorrow, the coach will leave from just outside the station. And if you want to go for a drink at the end of our tour today, there are plenty of cafés just behind the station.

We're still waiting for a few people, but while we wait I can tell you a little about the theatre. Although the building is very modern, in fact a theatre has existed on this site for over two hundred years. The original theatre used to be very popular because of the musicals it put on. However, it had to be rebuilt after a fire. Some people love the striking modern design, others hate it. These days, its popularity is mainly due to the fact that it attracts a lot of well-known performers.

Now, in a few minutes time – at 9.30 – we'll be starting our tour. First we're going to make our way down to Market Place, which is one of the most famous squares in the city – that should take us about 10 minutes. There's not too much traffic on the roads, so we should get there at quarter to ten at the latest.

Market Place was the city's old food market. People used to come in from the countryside to sell their fresh fruit and vegetables. Remember that these were the days before supermarkets! You won't find any food here now though. It's now a craft market and I think you'll find lots to interest you – especially if you want to take presents home. You'll see all kind of things like hand-painted local pottery and leather goods. Personally, I suggest that you visit the jewellery stalls. You really won't find anything like it anywhere else! But if you're looking for clothes, I'm afraid you'll be disappointed. Wait for this afternoon's visit.

We'll stop at the Market Place for an hour and a half and then continue the tour with a visit to the Regional Food Centre. Here you can find over fifty types of local cheeses! There is also fresh fruit juice on sale – orange juice, peach juice, pomegranate juice, produced in the villages of the region, and local jam too. You're welcome to buy things to take home with you, but the real reason for our visit is lunch. The idea is that you buy food and drink from the stalls and take it to eat in the lovely open-air dining area.

And finally, in the afternoon we will be visiting the Fashion Fair in the exhibition centre on the outskirts of the city. This is a huge venue, so try not to get lost. There is a whole hall devoted just to footwear – every kind of shoes and boots you can imagine. You can easily find it because it has a green roof. Just don't go through the blue doors at the entrance of the centre – you have to pay for that part of the exhibition. And if all that shopping has exhausted you, there's a café where you can rest your weary feet! That's in the building with a red sign. But don't worry, I'll remind you about all that later.

Right, everyone's here now, so, if you've all got your shopping bags, let's go!

1 A	2 C	3 B	4 A	5 A	6 B

SPEAKING

OUTCOMES

- talk about different experiences you might have when shopping
- plan your Part 2 talk using techniques for developing ideas
- express your feelings through intonation.

OUTCOMES

This lesson gives students further practice in preparing notes and speaking in Part 2. They will have the chance to activate topic-specific language learnt in other lessons of the unit. Some students may sound 'flat' when they speak making it difficult for the listener to understand their attitude to what they are saying. In this lesson they practise using intonation to sound positive or negative about what they are saying.

LEAD-IN

01 Elicit some of the vocabulary from previous lessons in the unit, e.g. mall, shopping centre, department stores, outdoor markets and supermarkets. If your class is weaker, you could also elicit some of the items they might shop for, e.g. (designer) clothes, jewellery or shoes.

Give students time to talk in pairs. The aim here is to get them talking so don't worry too much about accuracy.

02 This is a model of someone talking about shopping. It provides useful words and phrases, which students can use later. If you think it's necessary, you might choose to allow them a few minutes to look up the words in the box.

This exercise is also useful because students have to think about the grammar of the word and the kind of word needed in the gap, a task type they will meet in the reading paper. If students have print copies, ask them to write their answers in pencil, as they may have to make changes when they listen.

Give them plenty of time to study the text (even if they are not sure of which words go in which gaps) before listening. Students listen and check (more than once if needed).

Tapescript 46

The place where I really enjoy shopping is Covent Garden Market. It's very convenient because it isn't far from where I live. It isn't a traditional food market, though at one time it used to sell fruit and vegetables. Now, it's a collection of all sorts of independent shops and stalls. There's an amazing selection of things to buy – clothes, jewellery, books, art and crafts. I love it because it has a great atmosphere. There are cafés outside in the square, and often you can see street performers. It's very lively and friendly. I avoid the big malls because they're often out of the way – you need a car to get to them.

And what do I enjoy buying? Well, I'm keen on fashion and like to go clothes shopping whenever I can. I love trying on clothes even if I can't afford to buy them! And I love going to the sales! Sometime I manage to find great designer shoes at very reasonable prices. And I like shopping for really fun and original gifts for my friends – things that nobody else has. Covent Garden's a great place to do that.

1 convenient	2 traditional	3 all sorts of
4 selection	5 atmosphere	6 out-of-the-way
7 keen on	8 trying on	9 afford
10 reasonable	11 original	12 place

03 It is useful for students to make a note of antonyms as well as synonyms in their vocabulary notebook.

1 d	2 c	3 e	4 f	5 b	6 a

04 Students revisit the questions in exercise 1 armed with some new vocabulary.

Advice

After introducing a set of vocabulary, try to give students a chance to activate it (use it in a meaningful context) as soon as possible. This will aid memory as well as motivating them.

05 Students study the mind map for Daniel's talk and see if they can add anything to it by rereading the script.

Ask them to copy the mind map structure and headings and add their own notes based on their shopping preferences. Refer them to the tip reminding them that they have to do this very quickly so not to try and write full sentences.

Alternative

Show students the two types of notes (mind map and bullet points). Ask them which they prefer and why. One of the advantages of mind maps is that it is easier to add new information and identify connections between ideas.

06 By doing this, students can see how clear their notes are. Their partner should be able to use their notes to speak about the topic. Afterwards, they can give each other feedback about the clarity of their notes.

07 Tell students they are going to listen to a student doing a Task 2 talk and make notes. Tell them that they will have to recreate the talk from their notes so they should be clear and complete. Ask them to decide if they want to do a mind map or bullet points before they start listening.

Give them time to read the task card carefully.

Tapescript 47

You asked me to describe a place I like going shopping, so I'm going to talk about a department store in my town. It's called Judies and it's a very old store. In fact, it's about a hundred years old, so it's very famous. I would say that it's a landmark because everyone knows it. It's very large and spacious too, with four floors and more than thirty different departments to visit. You can find anything you want here, such as unusual presents for your friends, and you can buy really good food too. For example, you can buy traditional cakes and sweets that are famous in my area and they are delicious. It's an amazing shop but it's not cheap. In fact, it's one of the most expensive shops in the area.

I think it's in a good location because it's right in the centre of the town, which is very convenient. It's also very close to the railway station and a multi-storey car park too, so that's good for you if you have lots of shopping bags to carry.

What do I like to do there? Well, I really like spending time in the jewellery department and this is on the ground floor of the building. I love looking at the different rings and necklaces. I enjoy trying them on too! I like gold jewellery the best but I can't afford it.

Why do I like it so much? Well, I like the atmosphere in the store because it's very traditional. All the sales assistants are very friendly and helpful too. Yes, it's a really good store, so that's why I spend a lot of time in it!

Sample notes

What kind of place?: department store – 100 years old, famous, 4 floors, 30 departments

Where?: centre of town – near car park, station

What I like: jewellery department – rings, necklaces, gold

Why I like it: atmosphere – traditional, assistants friendly, helpful

08 Students work in pairs to give Yunmi's talk. This should help them evaluate their own note-making techniques. The pairs work together to look at the audio-script and see whether both of them had most of Yunmi's points.

What, if anything, do they need to improve about their notes?

You will have looked at most students' notes while monitoring, so add any points that commonly apply to students.

09 Decide if it would be useful for students to change partners.

Ask them if they have decided which note-taking method to use.

Feedback

Ask them to give feedback to their partners. You can move around listening to different students and highlight any common errors at the end.

Alternative

As they are still in the early stages of preparation, you might want to give them extra time for both writing notes and answering the questions so that they have the time they need to formulate what they want to say. You can work gradually on cutting down the time.

10 It is possible to predict which ones will be positive and which negative from the words but the aim here is for students to notice the intonation patterns. Generally when we sound positive or enthusiastic we have a wider pitch range and we sound flatter when we are negative.

Students generally enjoy copying intonation patterns so make sure they all join in.

11 This activity should also be enjoyable for students. They should sound different when they are just reading and when they use the appropriate intonation.

> **Alternative**
>
> Students could try reading the negative sentences sounding positive and vice versa and see if their partners could still decide if they were trying to sound positive or negative.

EXAM SKILLS

12 Students work in pairs to prepare and give a talk.

> **Alternative**
>
> For a strong class, change the topic or give different topics to each member of the pair.

> **Feedback**
>
> Circulate while students are doing the task and make a note of common errors.
>
> If technology allows, and your class is not too large, they could send you their recordings for thorough feedback. Complete a feedback form, for example.

Task fulfilment
Grammar
Vocabulary
Pronunciation
Overall

Don't give grades but write developmental comments, such as 'You used 'good' several times. Try to use different words instead' or 'Remember to pronounce 's' at the end of words clearly.

READING

OUTCOMES

- skim a text to find information quickly
- answer *True/False/Not Given* questions
- complete a summary of a text.

OUTCOMES

The topic of leisure is one that students are likely to encounter in at least one of the papers. The lessons of this unit will build their vocabulary in this very important area. The reading lesson introduces the 'True, False, Not Given' task type which students often worry about. By introducing a method of tackling this task type, we aim to reduce their anxiety and help them see it as just another type of task. The 'complete a summary' task type requires students to both understand the relevant section of the text and identify what part of speech is needed in the gaps.

LEAD-IN

01 Students identify the sports in the pictures. Check pronunciation.

| A baseball | B martial arts (Wu Shu) | C hockey |
| D table tennis | E rugby | |

02 Make sure students know the 9 sports. Check the meaning of 'earn', 'racket' and 'tackle'.

1 hockey: a, b, c, i, j, l	2 tennis: e, g, i, k
3 volleyball: a, e, i, h	4 football: a, b, c, i, j, l
5 rugby: a, i, j, l	6 baseball: a, f, i
7 table tennis: e, g, i, f	8 martial arts: d
9 basketball: a, c, i	

Read the instructions out to students, as they need to match each sport with more than one description. This exercise will work best in pairs as students might disagree about the answers.

03 All of these sports use the verb 'play', except 'martial arts' (do martial arts). Model the responses, for example:

'I've played tennis but I haven't played hockey'. (Past)

'I would like to play table tennis but I wouldn't like to play baseball' (Conditional)

Extension

A stronger class could give their opinions on the sports, e.g. I wouldn't like to play rugby because it looks dangerous'.

04 It is important to get students into the habit of reading a text very quickly to get the main ideas. For a weaker class, you could slightly increase the time limit, for example, giving them 90 seconds instead of a minute.

After the reading time is up, show students how they could use the given phrases, e.g.

There was something about a game played on horses.

I don't remember the details but it involved running around trying to catch other people.

There's a game, which is a bit like rock-paper-scissors.

Ask students to cover the text and tell their partner what they can remember.

Elicit the structure of the text, i.e. that each paragraph is about a different unusual sport from a different country. Understanding the structure from the beginning will help them locate information later.

05 Most of the sentences are paraphrases of part of the descriptions of the sports. Point out that the word 'Olympic' in sentence 1 is a name so will probably be found in the text. Get them to scan the text for the word 'Olympic(s)'.

For questions 01 to 04, students locate the correct paragraph as quickly as possible.

| 1 B | 2 E | 3 A | 4 C | 5 D |

Alternative

You could set this up as a race between individuals or groups.

06 This exercise gives students practice of the traditional True or False questions, before introducing the 'Not Given' element.

| 1 False | 2 True | 3 True | 4 False | 5 False |

07 This is an important Tip and activity because students typically waste time going through the whole text looking for the information. By understanding the organisation of the text, students should be able to predict where the information should be if it is there. In this case there is no information in paragraph C about the gender of players. If it were there, it would be in paragraph C.

| Not given |

08 This exercise is part of a gradual build up to the full True, False, Not Given activity. In this exercise, the statements are either True or Not Given. Remind students that information will be in the paragraph in which that sport is described or it will not be in the passage at all.

| 1 NG | 2 NG | 3 T | 4 T | 5 NG |

09 Students should now be ready to have a go at the True, False, Not Given task type. Remind them they may be looking for paraphrases of the given sentences.

After students have completed the exercise, go through the answers carefully, especially if they have got any wrong.

1 True	2 False	3 Not given
4 Not given	5 False	6 True

10 Tell students that the summary completion task involves both comprehension of the text and grammatical awareness. They need to read the instructions carefully as the missing words will either be given in a box or students will be told to find a word from the text.

2 G (mixed)	3 D (feature)	4 E (horses)
5 B (change)	6 C (clever)	

The example in the box demonstrates the process that students should go through when doing the summary completion task type.

Do question 2 with the students. Elicit that the missing word is a verb and the verbs in the box are 'change', 'feature' (also a noun), 'join', 'mixed' and 'moving'. Point out that these verbs are in different forms. That is another clue. Elicit the form of the verb that is needed (past tense). Elicit that the only possible answer is 'mixed'. Does that match the text? (Yes).

Students work individually on the rest of the exercise. If they get any answers wrong, refer them back to the process.

GRAMMAR FOCUS: COMPARATIVES

11 Point out the forms of the comparative adjectives (fast-faster, dangerous- more dangerous). Students will need to refer back to the text to do this. There are several possible answers but make sure their choices make sense in the context of the passage.

Students' own answers

EXAM SKILLS

12 Before students start the activity, refer them to the strategies listed at the end. Depending on your class, you may decide to give a time limit of 20-25 minutes or let them do it in their own time. If you want to check their progress, do it in class, but it can also be done as homework if time is short.

1 False	2 Not given	3 True
4 True	5 False	6 Not given
7 False	8 True	9 H (moving)
10 M (traceurs)	11 C (competition)	12 E (creativity)
13 B (barriers)	14 D (conflicts)	15 I (personal)

WRITING

OUTCOMES

- organise and write a Part 2 essay
- compare two different time periods
- link and signpost your ideas.

OUTCOMES

In this lesson, students continue to develop their topic-related vocabulary on leisure activities. They will be introduced to phrases that are commonly used with past and present tenses as well as some common linking expressions, which can be used in any task 2 essay. They are encouraged to develop their own opinions around the topic.

LEAD-IN

Collocation

This is two or more words that are habitually used together.

01 The collocations in this exercise are ones that students commonly make mistakes with. Point out that these expressions should be learnt as a 'chunk'. For example, while 'go to cinema' will be understood, it is incorrect and will lose them marks in the speaking or writing tests. Give students a chance to use these phrases in a meaningful way. Model some of the phrases, ensuring, that students use enjoy +ing, e.g. I enjoy going for a walk (or for walks). I don't enjoy going to the gym. Students practise the language in pairs.

1 go running / go for a run
2 go to the cinema
3 see a film / watch a film
4 visit friends / visit some friends
5 play sport / play sports
6 join a club
7 go walking / go for a walk (*slight difference in meaning*)
8 go to the gym

02 Read the essay question with students. Ask them if they agree or disagree. Elicit a few reasons before they read the essay. After they read it, elicit what is good about it. Don't guide them to the correct answers as exercise 3 does that.

The essay is well organised with an introduction, two main paragraphs and a conclusion. It is clear and easy to follow.

03 Students work through the questions in pairs. Generally it is a good essay apart from the grammatical errors.

1 Yes	2 Yes	3 Yes	4 Yes
5 Yes	6 Not always	7 Yes	

04 The errors the student has made are with tenses and verb forms. They are typical of the kind of errors students make at this level. Students can work alone to try and correct them. Refer them back to the relevant grammar in earlier units. When they've finished, ask them to check their answers with a partner. If they have different answers they should explain their choices.

> *are saying* – say   *explained* – will explain   *people less active* – people are less active   *go* – went / used to go   *we playing* – we play   *were walking* – walked / used to walk   *do* – did / used to do   *are become* – are becoming   *are not going* – don't go   *took* – takes   *I am agree* – I agree

GRAMMAR FOCUS: COMPARING PAST AND PRESENT

05 Explain to students that certain time phrases are used with certain tenses. Knowing this should help them choose the most appropriate tense when they are writing or speaking. In IELTS writing and speaking, students will often have to compare the situation now with the situation in the past. These time phrases, used with the correct tenses, will be helpful.

Extension

Get students to make up their own sentences using the given time phrases and the correct tense, e.g. Nowadays the weather is very bad.

Present	Past
now	before
nowadays	in the past
in today's world	several years ago
these days	there used to be

06 Remind students of the comparative forms they met in the reading lesson. They might need to use comparatives in writing task 1 or task 2. They might want to compare the situation in the past and present or in two different parts of the world.

This exercise exposes students to some of the common errors made in this area. For example, sometimes they forget to indicate the comparison, e.g. Now it is dangerous than before, or indicating it twice, e.g. Life is more harder than it used to be.

Another common error is forming comparatives with two syllable adjectives, as students are not sure which to use.

Moderner Incorrect

More modern=Correct

More funny-Incorrect

Funnier-Correct.

Remind students that two-syllable adjectives ending in 'y' generally cut the 'y' and add 'ier'. Those not ending in 'y' usually use more +adjective. However, there are exceptions.

Extension

For further practice, you could ask students to compare their own leisure activities in the past or present either orally or in writing. E.g. I ran faster when I was younger.

1 more expensive	2 harder	3 healthier
4 more dangerous	5 faster	

07 This exercise introduces some more linking expressions for different purposes. Students could highlight them in a different colour. Encourage students to use them in their own essays.

1 In my opinion, in my view, I agree that
2 on the other hand, however
3 There are points for and against this idea.
4 To sum up
5 the main reason

08 Get students to work in groups to brainstorm ideas for this essay topic. As a group they make two lists. Tell them to write in note form rather than complete sentences so that they focus on ideas not language.

Alternative

Divide the class into two and have one group make a list of advantages and the other group make a list of disadvantages.

09 Students read the essay ignoring the gaps to see if their ideas were mentioned. They complete the gaps and compare with a partner before you elicit the answers from the whole class.

Elicit what the student's own opinion is. He or she has chosen a moderate rather than an extreme position. Ask students what other positions the student could have adopted.

Extension

Students write their own conclusion to the essay.

1 my own opinion
2 Firstly
3 Thirdly
4 Unfortunately
5 One reason is that
6 In addition
7 also
8 My own view is

EXAM SKILLS

10 Check students understand 'compulsory'. Ask whether sports lessons are/were compulsory in their schools.

Students should decide if the sentences agree or disagree with the statement. Point out that the question asks them to decide on their opinion and state it at the beginning.

11 Students write the essay following the given plan either in class or for homework.

Alternative

Ask students to get into two groups depending on whether they agree or disagree with the statement. They work in small groups or pairs of like-minded classmates to write the essay. They exchange essays with a pair or group who wrote the essay with the opposite view.

Nowadays young people often spend their free time at home watching TV or playing computer games. Very few do sports outside of school. This means that if they don't do exercise during school time, they will be unfit and suffer from health problems. I agree that children should do sports lessons at school. In this essay I will explain why.

Some people say that sports lessons are a waste of time. Students have to prepare for exams and should spend all their time on academic work. This is what many people think in my country. In my opinion they are wrong. A healthy mind needs a healthy body. Doing exercise every day makes you happy and relaxed. Studying all the time can make you stressed.

Another reason for my opinion is that having an unfit generation will cause many problems for society. When today's children get older, unfortunately they may suffer from illnesses like heart disease. The government will have to spend a lot of money on doctors and hospitals. It is much better to create a fit and healthy adult population by getting children to do sports when they are still at school. In addition, sports teach people discipline and working as a team. This will help them in their future life.

In conclusion, I can say that prevention is better than cure. Children who do sports will be healthier, happier adults. They are more likely to continue with their active lifestyle when they grow up. In this way we can make a better society for the future.

12 This checklist can be used for self and peer evaluation.

Feedback

Use the checklist in exercise 12 to give feedback to students.

Use students' errors to create a version of the essay for students to correct in the next class.

Pay particular attention to the use of linking expressions and time phrases. Use ticks when students have used them appropriately.

LISTENING

OUTCOMES

- understand a description of a place
- follow directions
- label a map
- recognise distractors.

OUTCOMES

In the IELTS listening students may need to label a map, understand descriptions of places or follow directions to a place. The lesson follows the theme of the unit by introducing places associated with leisure time. The lesson also provides more practice in identifying distractors.

LEAD-IN

01 Students work in pairs to match the phrases to the pictures. What other phrases do they know for giving directions?

1 turn right	2 go straight ahead / straight on
3 turn left	4 go past
5 next to	6 opposite
7 in front of	8 behind

Examples of other words and phrases: go over/across (the bridge), drive along, pass, come to / get to / reach, on the other side of

02 Students listen to their partner carefully, correcting any errors in prepositions, etc. Move around the class monitoring and collate any common errors on the board.

Alternatives

Hide an item somewhere in the room. Ask a student to follow your directions to find the item. E.g. 'Go past Danny's desk, turn right at Anne's table, go straight on until you get to the window. Check behind the curtain.

Create a set of instructions for the whole class to follow. This could send students on a short route around the school, if appropriate. Ask stronger students to create their own directions to try out on the class.

03 Before students look at the words in the box, elicit some of the features shown on the map (e.g. houses, park, river, forest, school, shops). Check meaning of 'surgery' (doctor's office). Students match the pictures to the words.

You might want to teach the word 'landmarks': notable features, which help you find your way. Some will be general words like the ones given and others may be famous buildings in a particular town. Elicit how you would direct someone in the town/area of the city where you are. What are the major landmarks?

The map shows the streets and places in a small town.

1 roundabout	2 park	3 traffic lights
4 pond	5 zebra crossing	6 crossroads
7 river	8 bridge	

Examples of other useful places: railway station, bus stop, cinema, statue, fountain

04 Ask students to look at the map and decide which letters could be Main Street and Silver Street (B, D, G, J or K). They listen and check.

Tapescript 49

Melissa: Thanks for offering to drive us all to the concert. It's really kind of you and makes getting there much easier. I don't live far from you at all. First, you need to turn right onto Maple Avenue and drive to the bottom of the road, passing the supermarket on your left. Then, you need to turn left at the traffic lights and then take a sharp right onto Main

Street. You can also go straight on here, past the surgery, but I usually drive down Main Street. Follow this road until you reach a roundabout – you'll pass a park and some shops on your right. When you get to the roundabout, take the first turning on the left, onto Silver Street. As you approach the crossroads here, my house is the first on the corner.

1 G	2 D	3 C

Again, narrow down the choices by asking which letters could be Melissa's house (A, C, E, F, H, I). They listen again to identify her house.

05 Students listen twice and choose the letters.

If students have had difficulty with exercises 4 and 5, give them time to read the audio-script and/or listen again with the audio-script in front of them.

Tapescript 50

Melissa: Sorry, I've just remembered, I told Sarah you would collect her on the way. Forget the route I just gave you, I'll give you another set of directions. This route might even be easier. Again, you need to turn right onto Maple Avenue, and go up to the lights. Instead of turning left here, turn right, with the park on your left. Then after the zebra crossing, take the first turning on your left onto New Road. Drive along New Road until you reach the bridge. Sarah's house is the second house after the bridge. That's on the right; there are shops on the left. Once you've picked up Sarah, take the first turning on the left, onto Silver Street, and go straight ahead until you reach the roundabout. Go straight ahead at the roundabout and then take the first turning on the right, Oak Avenue. My house is number 1. It's on the corner.

4 K	5 H	6 B

06 Remind students of the meaning of 'distractor'. Tell students that there will always be distractors and they should expect them. It is useful for students to study a range of forms the distractors might take. For example, the speaker might correct him/herself 'Sorry, I meant on the right'. Or use a phrase like 'Instead of turning left, turn right'.

The distractors are:

(Question 1) *You can also go straight on here*

(Question 4) *Instead of turning left here*

(Question 5) *there are shops on the left.*

07 Point out that the words on the list, which are not correct answers will be mentioned in the audio-script. Again, it might be useful for students to study the audio-script

because there are more examples of distractors, such as 'there used to be a cinema there'.

Tapescript 51

Tanya: Hi Jane, this is Tanya. I'm calling to make arrangements for the concert on Saturday. I can't believe you've never been to the Arena before. I often go at the weekend. There isn't just the Arena concert venue, there are also lots of other things to do: shopping, restaurants, exhibitions. I'm giving Melissa and Sarah a lift, so shall we all meet up for a coffee before the concert? I'll give you directions. OK, listen carefully.

As you walk through the main entrance, you come to a square with a big fountain in the middle. This is where people usually arrange to meet up and sometimes they have live music here. Beyond the square, on Main Avenue, on your right, there are several restaurants, and opposite these on your left is an exhibition centre. There used to be a cinema here, but they moved it when they finished building the arena.

So there are several coffee shops to choose from, one near the fountain and one in the north end of the building, but I suggest that we go to the one at the end of Main Avenue, because it'll probably be less busy than the others. It's right at the end, after you pass the art gallery on the right. So shall we all meet there at seven o'clock?

Then after we've had a coffee, to get into the Arena we just need to go through the shopping centre, which will be on our right once we go back down Main Avenue. It can be a bit tempting, but there's no other way to get there, as the Arena is the other side of it. Oh, and there are toilets beside the entrance if you need them. And then after the concert, they open the door opposite and you can go straight out into the car park, which is very convenient.

Let me know if you can make it for seven. I'm looking forward to seeing you – it's been a while.

1 F	2 A	3 H	4 G

08 This exercise practises locating places on a different type of map- a campsite. Help students with words they need to talk about the map, e.g. lake, tents. Get them to predict the activities that might be mentioned. Elicit cycling, playing sports (which ones?), boating, doing archery (the targets should make the meaning clear or you could mime it). It doesn't matter if the activities they come up with are mentioned or not- try to get them predicting what they may hear. Write the activities up on the board.

09 Point out that the activities will include a gerund ('ing' form). Check students' spellings of the words.

Tapescript 52

First of all, welcome to our activity summer camp. I hope you enjoy all the activities we have on offer. We start our tour at the outdoor theatre here, where we hold many of our evening activities. From here you can see our various watersport activities. Directly in front of the campsite, on the edge of the lake, we have the kayaking centre. And then in front of the beach, we have an area reserved for diving. Swimming isn't permitted here.

If you like racket sports, just behind the beach you can practise badminton in the large building. That's quite popular in the evenings. We also have some outdoor tennis courts. We used to have basketball in the building too, but now you can play it on the court behind the building. And if these activities make you hungry, the path from there takes you straight to the café and dining hall.

However, we'll continue our walk along the lake shore and I'd like to draw your attention to two other areas. One is this part of the lake, which is perfect for swimming, but, for safety reasons, only when an instructor is present. Unfortunately we can't offer sailing as an option here this year. And I also want to point out, just across the lake, a track for cycling. Some people in the past have also gone running on the track, but there were a few accidents because there isn't enough space for runners and cyclists, so now running isn't allowed. So now let's take this path here, towards the tennis courts. On our left, you can see there's a football field. Gary's our coach and he'll be organising tournaments during the week. He'll arrive tomorrow, because he's taking part in a rugby game today.

And now if we walk up to the right of the tennis courts, we can see the archery field, surrounded by trees. And in the building just to the right of this, you can hire equipment for the archery and buy snacks and drinks. It also has some table tennis tables, so you can go there and have a game if the weather turns bad.

1 diving	2 badminton	3 basketball
4 swimming	5 cycling	6 football
7 table tennis		

EXAM SKILLS

10 Elicit from students what they should do during their preparation time (study the map and think of how different areas might be referred to). Point out the compass in the corner. This indicates that the speaker might use compass points to explain where things are.

Point out that while there are 8 questions, there are 13 labelled points on the map so some of the letters won't be used.

How you follow up the exercise will depend on how the students have done. If they have got confused, tell them to go through the audio-script carefully while following the map.

Tapescript 53

Good morning. I'd like to thank the council for agreeing to this meeting and for welcoming us here today to explain to you all our plans for Pine Woods Centre. Our aim is to make Pine Woods a place where people of all ages can come and enjoy their free time. The centre will feature our Tree Tops Challenge – only for the brave and fearless! For the less brave, and for families with children, there will be adventure playgrounds, indoor and outdoor, and a feeding area for farm animals and we will also offer cycle trails through the woods.

I'll give you an overview of Pine Woods first and then tell you more about each area in more detail. This first slide shows the overall layout of the centre and where all the activities will be situated. As you can see from the map, the entrance to this attraction will be on the south side. As visitors enter from the car park, they will walk along this path leading them to the café and gift shop. The gift shop will be where tickets are on sale and therefore needs to be near the entrance. So this building here on the right will be the café and the building on the left will be the gift shop. There will also be a picnic field behind the café for the warmer months. It's the area just to the right of the café as you look at the map. And in the bottom right-hand corner of the picnic field we're planning to have a barbecue area, where people can hire a barbecue and bring their own food to cook. It'll be great for parties. In summer we plan to have bands performing here in the evenings.

To the west of the gift shop is where the Tree Tops Challenge will take place. There is a path here winding through the forest, and up in the trees there will be all sorts of high-level adventure apparatus – rope swings, awesome rope bridges and tunnels, and zip wires where you can fly way above the forest floor. This adventure experience will only be open to those aged 15 and over.

Beyond the Tree Tops Challenge there will be an adventure playground. To get to it, you go along this path from the entrance until you reach the crossroads, then you turn left. The young children's playground will have a fence around it, making it safer and keeping them away from the lake. The indoor play area, only for the very young, will be on the east side of the farm, near the café and just inside the picnic area.

And finally, let's turn our attention back to this area here, where the paths meet and form a crossroads. This path leading to the east end of the farm will take our visitors to the area which houses the farm animals. Children will be able to watch the animals being fed and cared for, and in some instances they will be able to feed the animals themselves. The sheep will be in this first area on the right here, directly opposite the pigs, and the goats will go at the very end there. We haven't quite decided on the other areas yet.

So those are our plans. We hope they will be approved, and we look forward to welcoming you back in the not too distant future to see the final result.

| 1 J | 2 L | 3 M | 4 I | 5 B | 6 F | 7 G | 8 E |

SPEAKING

OUTCOMES

- use positive and negative adjectives to talk about free-time activities
- recognise and use linking words in your talk (Speaking Part 2)
- pronounce weak forms of words
- give a complete talk and assess your own performance (Speaking Part 2).

OUTCOMES

This lesson gives students practice in completing a Task two task and evaluating their own performance. As students need to speak for up to two minutes in Part two, they will need to be able to link their ideas together in different ways. Previous lessons in the unit have introduced vocabulary for free-time activities; this lesson builds on this by presenting some adjectives that can be used to describe the activities.

LEAD-IN

01 Before students pair up for the discussion, elicit the names of the activities shown in the pictures. Refer them to the tip. Remind them of the sports mentioned in the reading lesson, if applicable (play volleyball, do martial arts)

02 Check meanings of the adjectives in the box. Refer students to the example sentences. Which words can replace 'excellent' in the second example? (great, brilliant). Monitor and point out any strange uses of the adjectives.

03 Ask students what the words in the box have in common (they are all negative). Tell students they will use them to talk about negative aspects of sports or sports they don't like or are not good at. Refer to the pictures for more examples.

04 Ask students to look at the picture and elicit 'ballroom dancing'. Have students tried it or watched it? What do they know or think about it? Students listen to the talk and follow the audio-script. Check the meaning of tango, samba and flamenco, with pictures if possible.

Tapescript 54

> I'm going to talk about a hobby I'd like to take up in the future. I really want to learn ballroom dancing. This is because I love Latin music and I love the way the dancers move and shake. I also want to give myself a challenge and learn something new. Watching ballroom dancing always makes me feel excited. I don't think it'll be too dificult for me, because I already do ballet and tap dancing. I like learning new steps. For example, I really want to learn the tango or the samba because these are exciting and look good to people watching. I've tried Flamenco dancing but I'm not very good. I'm also worried about finding the right dance partner, because I'll be a little slow to learn in the beginning. So I might fall over sometimes. In fact I'll probably fall over quite a lot!

Alternative

Students could listen once without the audio-script (ask them to cover it). After they listen, ask them questions about it such as:

Why does she want to learn ballroom dancing?

How does she feel when she watches ballroom dancing?

What problems does she think she might have with this activity?

05 Students should not look back at the audio-script but use logic and the linkers to match up the phrases. Tell them these and other linkers are useful for the Part 2 task.

Students might not be familiar with 'in fact'. It is used to give more evidence for the statement. Give a few more examples, such as 'I love going on social media. In fact I spend several hours a day on it.'

| 1 F | 2 D | 3 B | 4 C | 5 E | 6 G | 7 A |

06 Students work in pairs to practise using the linkers in context. Suggest they take it in turns to go through the list. They can talk about any free-time activity, not just the ones in the box.

07 If possible show a picture of an acoustic guitar by way of introduction to the activity. Students work alone to choose the correct linker. They can check with a partner before they listen and check.

Give students a chance to read the script again and ask about any unknown language. Point out that 'take up the guitar' means to start learning to play the guitar.

Transcript 55

I'm going to tell you about a leisure activity I'd like to do in the future. I'd really like to learn how to play the acoustic guitar. This is because I love music and I love the beautiful sound this kind of guitar makes. I also want to give myself a challenge and learn something new. I don't think it'll be too difficult for me because I already know how to read music. I play the piano but I'm not very good. I think playing the guitar will be easier. I also like the fact that you can carry a guitar round easily and play it anywhere. For example I can play it in the park or on the beach.

I can't think about learning it at the moment because I'm too busy. I need to focus on my studies and prepare for my exams. I think that I'd like to take up the guitar next year. All my exams will be over by then, so I'll have more time, and more money too. In fact, I'll need money to pay for lessons! I think that learning the guitar would change my life in a positive way. If I learn to play it really well, I'll start my own band. I'd love to perform live on stage at a concert. I think that would be fantastic!

Extension

Ask students to highlight the adjectives used in the talk (there are at least 7). What do they describe?

1	because	2	and	3	also	4	and
5	because	6	but	7	also	8	For example
9	or	10	because	11	and	12	so
13	In fact						

Transcript 56

Examiner: Do you generally enjoy trying new things?

Candidate 1: Yes, I would say I like to try new things, meet new people. It's something that is very important to me.

Examiner: Is there any other activity you would like to try one day?

Candidate 2: Yes, I've always thought about windsurfing, I mean, I'm a big fan of the ocean and love water sports, so it's next on my list of things to do.

08 Refer students to the tip. Tell students that they might be asked a follow-up question. They should not give a very extended answer but nor should they just say two or three words.

09-10 Both word stress and sentence stress cause problems for students. These exercises raise awareness of the way stress works in English. There are several ways to demonstrate the rhythm of the sentences. Clap or bang the table to show the stressed words. Get students to do the same.

Tapescript 57

to:	I want to go now.
and:	You have to wear a shirt an' tie.
a:	Wait a minute.
of:	Get me a glass of water.
some:	Will you lend me some money?
for:	This is for you.
from:	I come from London

1 I want to learn to play the guitar.
2 I enjoy playing football and baseball.
3 I bought a new golf club.
4 I would like to learn to play chess.
5 I need some driving lessons.
6 I played drums in a band for a long time.
7 I plan to cycle from the north of Africa to the south.

EXAM SKILLS

11 Remind students what they learnt about making notes in previous units. Give them a minute to make notes.

Alternative

After one minute, stop them and get them to evaluate their notes. Give them another minute to improve them.

12 Encourage students to peer evaluate as this is good practice for evaluating themselves. You might need to 'sell' students the idea of repeating the activity. Tell them it is a chance to improve their performance after peer/self evaluation.

This unit is about fame and the media. Various aspects of this topic may arise in any of the IELTS papers. Students will learn relevant vocabulary and engage with some common themes they may encounter in the IELTS examination.

READING

> **OUTCOMES**
>
> - match features of the passage
> - identify the writer's views
> - write first conditional sentences.

OUTCOMES

In the reading lesson they will learn how to approach two task types: matching features and Yes, No, Not Given, in which they need to be able to identify the writer's views rather than facts.

LEAD-IN

01 It is assumed that students, even those that lack a wide general knowledge, have a working knowledge of the internet. They may name local or international sites here.

> *Sample answers*
> 1 Google, Yahoo, Bing, MSN
> 2 BBC, CNN, New York Times, Yahoo News
> 3 Facebook, Twitter, Instagram, China: Weibo
> 4 Wikipedia, Britannica.com, Encyclopedia.com

02 Again, it is assumed that all students use the internet for a variety of purposes. Ask them what they spend most time doing online. What are their favourite sites?

> Students' own answers

03 Students should now be accustomed to skim reading. Tell them that the aim of their first quick reading of the text is to find the purpose of the passage. (A, B or C). Remind them they will have an opportunity to read the text in detail later.

> B

04 For the matching features task type, the text will contain reference to several people, places or things. In this case, the text refers to 5 social media platforms and the list A to E follows the order of the text. Point out that the list of sentences will not be in order. Go through steps 1 to 4 with students and help them identify the sentences that refer to YouTube. They should do the others on their own following the same steps.

> 1 E   2 D   3 C   4 B   5 A   6 A

05 Introduce the idea of fact versus opinion in any way that is suitable for your class. For example, (your town) has a population of around 500,000 (fact)/ (your town) is a good place to bring up children (opinion). Perhaps ask students to come up with their own facts and opinions about the town or school.

Stronger students could brainstorm other ideas to illustrate facts/opinions

Point out that sometimes writers express their views in a less direct way. For example, instead of saying 'He stood up. He was unhappy', they might write 'He stood up with a sigh.' The sign implies rather than states directly that the person was unhappy.

Students read the 3 sentences and decide which one contains a personal view. Ask them to justify their decision. By saying people 'waste their time' on Facebook, the writer is implying rather than stating his or her personal view.

> C The opinion is not stated directly, but the phrase 'waste their time' shows the writer doesn't like Facebook.

06 This exercise gives students a mini practice of the task type. Ask them what claims the writer makes (she is only a little bit famous, for example).

> **Claim**
>
> A claim is presented as a fact by the writer but without real evidence.

Get students to think of synonyms for the key words in the claims they have mentioned, e.g. famous-well-known.

Students do the exercise.

> 1 No   2 Yes   3 Not Given   4 No

Feedback

Point out that in the Not Given statement, coffee is mentioned, but it doesn't say or imply that the writer would like to drink more coffee. She is talking about an imagined situation (being very famous), not her real life.

07 Tell students that they are going to practise Yes, No, Not Given questions on the longer text they read earlier. In the exam, they should have skim read the passage before so they should have an idea where the information will be found. Ask them to identify the key words and decide if they are likely to be paraphrased. If so, can they think of any synonyms for the key words? A synonym for 'blog' probably won't 'be used, for example. 'Internet' also probably won't be replaced, but 'world wide web' or 'the web' is possible.

Refer students to the tip. Small words may be very important. 'Some' or 'all', for example can change the meaning.

> See exercise 08.

08 Ask students if their reasons for their answers were the same as the explanations given. If they got them wrong, make sure they now understand why.

09 Elicit how students will be able to locate the parts of the text they need to read carefully (they know the text is organised by social media platform, e.g. Facebook or Twitter. Elicit that 'vines' is a specific term so unlikely to be paraphrased. Elicit or explain that vines are very short video clips that people upload and share.

4 No	5 Not Given	6 Yes

GRAMMAR FOCUS: FIRST CONDITIONAL

10 Write the example sentence on the board. If possible, write the two clauses in different colours to make sure students are aware of the two clauses. Highlight 'if', 'want' and 'will need'. Tell students the second clause is called the 'result clause' as it gives the result of the condition being met.

Students should notice that one sentence has 'should' in the result clause as it is giving advice.

Extension

Give students some 'If' clauses to complete. They should be things that are likely to happen, such as

If I have time tomorrow,

If (local team) wins the match,

Let them share their completed sentences with the class.

If clause
If you want to become famous on YouTube,

Result clause
you should make lots of videos and release one every day.

If clause
If you allow advertisements in your videos,s
Result clause
you will make money.

If clause
If you achieve fame on Facebook,
Result clause
it probably won't last.

Should is used instead of *will/won't* in one of the result clauses.

With stronger students you could elicit other 'if' and 'result' clauses. They could perhaps brainstorm In pairs or small groups and then share with the class.

EXAM SKILLS

11 This text is organised in a similar way to the previous text in the unit, in that each paragraph describes one animal. Remind students to start with Hachiko and carefully read the paragraph about him. Then read all the statements carefully and decide which ones refer to him. Do the same for Knut and Elsa.

For questions 8-16, point out that as the first two questions do not refer to a specific animal, the statements are

more likely to be in the introduction or conclusion. This is something they could work out from skim reading the text.

1 A	2 C	3 B	4 B
5 C	6 A	7 B	8 No
9 Yes	10 No	11 Yes	12 Not Given
13 No	14 Not Given	15 Yes	16 No

WRITING

OUTCOMES

- avoid repeating words in your Part 2 essay
- develop a paragraph
- provide specific support for your main points.

OUTCOMES

In Part 2 of the writing paper, paragraphing is very important. Students will be penalised under 'Coherence and Cohesion', if their paragraphing is inadequate or missing. Tell students that in this lesson they will learn to organise and write a paragraph properly. In their Part 2 essays, students will need to provide 'specific' support. This means writing an example of the point they are making, such as an event they have read about or something they have experienced or heard about themselves. The ability to use a range of vocabulary is important in the writing paper. It is also a part of 'Cohesion' to be able to avoid repetition in different ways, including using pronouns.

LEAD-IN

01 The introductory activity presents useful vocabulary for the topic of fame and the media. Ask students to work in pairs and do as many as they can without using a dictionary. Point out that they can use 'clues', such as suffixes ('er' for people, 'ous' and 'y' for adjectives). If they use dictionaries, make sure they are aware that the dictionary will tell them the part of speech. Encourage the use of monolingual learners' dictionaries.

Lead feedback in a way that students are required to say the words. Indicate word stress to aid pronunciation, e.g. papa**razzi**

Nouns(things): media, newspaper, fortune, website
Nouns (people): reporters, photographers, celebrity, fan, model, paparazzi, blogger, star
Adjectives: wealthy, popular, talented, famous, well-known

02 Students read the title. Give them a few minutes to brainstorm (in groups) advantages and disadvantages.

Alternative

Half the class brainstorms advantages and the other half disadvantages. Have them then share whole class.

Point out that this essay would have a simple organisation pattern:

- General introduction
- Advantages
- Disadvantages
- Conclusion- your opinion

Tell students that the paragraph they are going to evaluate is the second, which contains the advantages. Does the writer mention any of the points they came up with?

Students work in pairs to find the good and bad points about the paragraph.

Elicit that the whole paragraph is about advantages. It has four advantages and each one is supported.

On the negative side, elicit that there is repetition of 'advantage' and 'famous'. Also, the first conditional is used too much. Although it is a good structure to use in this paragraph, it is better to use a range of structures.

> **Good things:** well organised, main points are clear, supporting evidence is given
>
> **Bad things:** repetition of key words

03 Students work individually to complete the table. Check their answers.

> **Point 2:** you have fans
>
> **Evidence:** they take photos of you, send you letters
>
> **Point 3:** don't have to wait in queues
>
> **Evidence:** you can go to the front
>
> **Point 4:** help good causes
>
> **Evidence:** others will also give to charity

04 Remind students that the student repeated the key words 'advantage' and 'famous'. Tell them that exercise 4 provides 3 synonyms each for those words. Students work individually to rewrite the paragraph, avoiding repetition of 'advantage' and 'famous'.

Alternative

If your class is strong, they could also change some of the first conditional sentences to other structures.

> Sample answer
>
> Fame has many advantages. *If you are well-known* you might also be wealthy. You can buy a big house and an expensive car. *Another benefit* is that you have fans. They take photographs of you and send you letters. *One more good point* is if you are *someone that everyone knows*, you don't have to wait in queues. You can go to the front. The last positive aspect of being famous is that you can use

> your fame and money for good causes. People will copy you and support charity too. In this way, you can make a real difference in the world.

05 The disadvantages paragraph has avoided the problem of repetition found in the advantages paragraph. Question 1 asks students to identify how this has been done.

Students could draw a table in their notebook like the one in exercise 03 to answers questions 02 and 03.

> 1 Disadvantages: uses pronouns (the main one) and similar words (drawback, negative aspect, problem)
>
> Famous: uses similar words (well-known, fame) and avoids using 'being famous' when it is not necessary (the main one, a final problem…)
>
> 2 1) You don't have a private life.
>
>   2) People say bad things about you.
>
>   3) Your family will suffer.
>
>   4) It is stressful.
>
> 3 1) Reporters follow you everywhere and take photos of you.
>
>   2) They even tell lies about you.
>
>   3) Your children may have paparazzi following them.
>
>   4) Some actors or singers are badly affected by the pressure.

06 Although the advantages and disadvantages paragraphs already studied have evidence, it is not always <u>specific</u> evidence. Point out that in an essay about fame and the media, the ideal would be to name celebrities who exemplify some of the points.

In this exercise, students add the specific support given in 1-3 into the paragraph in the most appropriate location.

> Sample answer
>
> There are also disadvantages of being famous. The main one is that you do not have a private life. Reporters follow you everywhere. Even if you are tired or sick they take photographs of you. Many celebrities have got into trouble after getting angry with reporters and photographers who were following them. The second drawback of being well known is people say bad things about you. They even tell lies about you. <u>Even people like Bill Gates, who gives most of his money to charity are criticized!</u> The third negative aspect of fame is your family will also suffer. Even your children may have paparazzi following them. <u>For example, everyone has seen pictures of Harper, the young daughter of David and Victoria Beckham.</u> A final problem is it is very stressful. Some actors or singers are badly affected by the pressure. <u>Many famous people have died young due to plane and car accidents, or have become sick due to overwork</u> and always being in public view.

07 Students work in pairs to do this. Ideally, they would have some information about the named person, such as approximately how much an actor earns per film or the net worth of a celebrity. This is why students preparing for

IELTS are encouraged to read newspapers, magazines and websites with all kinds of different information. Tell students to make up information if they do not have it as IELTS is not a truth or general knowledge test!

Check that students' examples support the points they are meant to support.

Sample answers

Famous people are often rich. Jackie Chan is worth $350 million.

You might have a lot of fans. Taylor Swift gets thousands of fan letters a week.

You can use your fame and money to help. Bill Gates donates most of his money to charity.

GRAMMAR FOCUS: PRONOUNS

08 Go through the examples with students. It is important that students are able to use different kinds of pronoun (including subject, object, possessive and demonstrative). Pronoun use is an important aspect of cohesion.

1 Fan Bingbing is a popular actress in China. <u>She</u> starred in My Fair Princess. (Also accept Fan Bingbing is a popular Chinese actress, <u>who</u> starred in My Fair Princess)

2 There are some reasons for my opinion. The first <u>one</u> is it is difficult to be famous.

3 Benedict Cumberbatch is one of my heroes. I met <u>him</u> when I was in London.

4 Our country has laws that protect people from paparazzi. Some country's laws are not as strict as <u>ours</u>.

09 Tell students that, 'to what extent' is a common question type in Part 2. Students need to be able to clearly state their opinion and support it with evidence, as well as presenting some arguments from the opposite side to show fairness.

A common problem for students is that they do have an opinion on a topic. Wide reading and reflection on what they have read (including in their own language) will be useful preparation. Tell students that the four opinions presented in this exercise are the best options. Saying 'I don't know what I think' is not an option!

Extension

Students with the same opinion (a, b, c or do) get together and find reasons for their opinion. They then present these to the rest of the class.

10 This exercise gets students to look at the essay as a whole, focusing on its structure as well as the specific support it presents.

Stress that the essay looks at both sides, even though the purpose of presenting the opposing side's arguments is to discredit them.

Point out that there is no one correct way to organise the essay. All the plans are possible. However, there must be a clear plan.

1 The writer agrees that taking photographs of under 18s should be banned.

2 The Beckham children, Prince William/George, Celebrities with ugly kids website

3 Yes. The writer understands that people are interested in seeing photos of celebrities and acknowledges (but rejects) the point of view, 'fame has a price'.

4 Plan 1

EXAM SKILLS

11 Students use the points given or others they can think of but must supply their own supporting evidence. Point out that there is no real difference between 'Do you agree or disagree?' and 'To what extent do you agree or disagree?' They can still say they agree or disagree strongly or 'tend to' agree or disagree.

Alternative

With a stronger class, you might choose not to give the points and have them come up with their own.

Sample essay

Every year Forbes a list of the highest paid celebrities is published. Some stars are paid hundreds of millions of dollars every year. Some people think they deserve this money for their talent and hard work. I personally disagree. I don't believe anyone should have such excessive amounts of money. In this essay I will explain the reasons for my view.

Some people argue that the highest earning celebrities are special. They have a talent that few of us possess and they have worked incredibly hard to become the best. My view is that we all have our own skills and abilities and most of us work hard. Just because someone's talent is for making things or teaching, why should they get paid so much less?

It is true that we create the demand for celebrities that lets them become so wealthy. However, I think we are all paying too much for tickets to concerts and sporting events. This is unfair because people with low incomes don't have the opportunity to see these events in person. If celebrities earned less, more people would be able to afford to buy music and go to concerts.

In addition, I think that it is bad for society that only singers, actors and sportsmen are valued. Children no longer want to grow up to be train drivers, carpenters, plumbers or even teachers because they want a 'celebrity lifestyle' of expensive houses and private jets.

To conclude, I strongly agree that famous people should have a lifestyle which is more similar to that of ordinary people.

(260 words)

Feedback

Give students credit for specific support, stating their own view clearly and briefly presenting the opposing view. Give feedback on paragraphing. Make sure each paragraph contains similar ideas. Tick the use of synonyms and pronouns.

LISTENING

OUTCOMES

- complete a flow-chart
- predict what information is missing in a flow-chart
- deal with technical or scientific flow-charts.

OUTCOMES

This lesson on flow chart completion focuses on the similarities with other types of gap-fill tasks students are already familiar with. It uses a positive approach- focusing on what students understand to help them overcome fear of tasks, which use unfamiliar technical or scientific language.

LEAD-IN

01 Students will probably know who Justin Bieber is. If not, ask them to describe the person in the picture- e.g. young, blond hair. If they don't know, let them guess how he became famous.

> 1 He is Justin Bieber, a famous singer and songwriter.
> 2 The answer is found in the recording for exercise 2.

02 Ask students to look at the first gap. Elicit that the missing word must be some kind of musical instrument. Ask what other instruments they know.

Ask students to look through the other gaps and decide what kind of word will go in each gap. They can make guesses based on the exact context. For example, what words go after ' enter talent'? (show, contest, competition)- there are a limited number of possible answers. This might not always be possible but at least they can predict the part of speech that will fill the gap.

Elicit the number of words that can be used in each gap (no more than two).

Allow students to listen twice if necessary.

Transcript 59

Justin Bieber's rise to fame is an interesting story. He was interested in music from a very early age and he taught himself how to play a whole selection of musical instruments, which I think is rare in youngsters these days. Like a lot of teenagers who want to be pop stars, he learned the guitar. But, whereas very few of those teenagers put in the effort needed to be successful, Bieber, on the other hand, not only learnt how to play the piano as well, but also mastered the drums and even the trumpet! One day he hopes to learn the violin.

He was clearly gifted, and his mother used to arrange for him to take part in local competitions. He came second in one, and his mother posted his performance on YouTube. She kept posting other clips of him singing, and soon these attracted a number of fans

who started following him, though at this point he still hadn't found fame.

His big break came when a music executive came across these videos by accident when he was looking for a performance by a different artist. He immediately recognised Bieber's talent and gave the teenager a contract with his recording company. His first record was a worldwide hit. He shot to fame in just two years and is now a global superstar, one of the most well-known performers the world has ever seen.

1 piano	2 competitions
3 fans	4 music executive
5 contract	6 (global) superstar

03 It would be useful for students to study the script at this point.

Point out that in the flow chart the 'missing' instrument is the first mentioned. However, in the script the guitar is mentioned first. In question 2, the word 'talent' is not mentioned in the script and 'take part in' replaces 'entered'.

1 No	2 Yes

Advice

Close study of the relationship between the questions and script is a useful way of developing the skills needed for the IELTS listening test.

04 Ask students if they would like to be famous. Why/why not?

As you read through the steps with the class, complete them for the first sentence with a gap. The key words are 'followed' and 'private life'. The word needs to follow 'by'. It must be a living thing, probably a person or people. Elicit 'fans'.

Students complete the gaps and compare with a partner.

1 verb	2 noun	3 adjective	4 noun
5 verb	6 adjective	7 adjective	8 verb

05 Students listen and check. Ask them if the predictions they made helped them.

Transcript 60

A: I wouldn't like to be famous. I would hate people to recognise me all the time. You would always be followed by journalists and never able to have a private life. Being followed on a good day, when you've been to the hairdresser and are wearing your best jeans, is perhaps acceptable, but can you imagine how it would make you feel on a bad day.

B: I would love to be famous. I would adore all the attention and the special treatment. Everywhere I went people would know my name and I wouldn't need to queue anymore. The best part though, would be meeting other famous people. I can imagine that would be so interesting. They would come to my private yacht and I would visit their mansions.

1 recognise	2 journalists	3 acceptable	4 attention
5 queue	6 interesting	7 private	8 visit

06 Point out that students need to use clues to make predictions. They should read the entire flow chart stage. For example, in stage 4, 'You can learn from the experience' implies that the stage is referring to failure.

1 verb	2 noun	3 noun	4 verb

07 Again, students reflect on how successful their predicting was.

Transcript 61

Interviewer: So, you've been a famous singer for over three decades now. What advice would you give to someone wanting to become famous?

Celebrity: Well, my first piece of advice is – don't try and become famous. Instead focus on being good at something. Choose something you enjoy and then work hard at doing well in that area.

Interviewer: What did you do to become such a successful singer?

Celebrity: Well, a good way to be the best is to learn from the experts. Find people you admire in your area of interest. Try to get as close to them as possible. Observe them carefully. If possible, talk to them. Ask lots of questions. Don't copy them, but try to learn from them. And don't be afraid to experiment, try something new.

Interviewer: Being the best is one thing, but how did you get yourself known?

Celebrity: Getting yourself known is indeed another skill you must work on. One thing is for sure, nobody is going to come to you. You have to make opportunities for yourself. You have a product to sell and the product is you. It is much easier to do that these days, especially with the internet around. Many people use social media for this.

Interviewer: Any other piece of advice?

Celebrity: Yes, the last thing I would say is, if you want to be really successful in something, you will most likely experience a certain amount of failure. People who fail at some point often say that the experience has been a great lesson and helped them on the road to success. Try to learn from these moments instead of being frightened of them. In fact, some of the most successful people have often failed countless times before reaching their end goal. What makes them successful, is that they kept on trying regardless.

1 work (hard)	2 (the) experts	3 opportunities	4 fail

08-09 The techniques we have been looking at can also help when students are faced with flow charts containing technical or scientific language that they are unfamiliar with. Point out that the technical terms are often explained in the text.

Get students to highlight key words they understand in the 4 stages. The aim of this is to build confidence. They probably know enough to get the answer in spite of not knowing some key vocabulary.

Tell students that the technical language such as that highlighted will be used in the text so they have to listen for that rather than a synonym or paraphrase. This should also build confidence.

For this task, the options are given. Students use grammar and meaning to predict which words go in each gap. Ask them to check with a partner.

08

1 adjective	2 adjective	3 adjective	4 noun
5 adjective	6 adjective	7 adjective	

09

1 **G** manual	2 **J** useful	3 **C** closer	4 **E** light
5 **B** brighter	6 **H** popular	7 **F** long	

10 By listening, students narrow down the choices from the options they selected during the prediction stage. Remind them that some of the words are distractors.

Tapescript 62

If you're going to take filmmaking seriously, you need to learn how to get the best from your camcorder. Many people use camcorders these days, to take short videos of their friends and family, and often people just use the automatic functions. These work well enough for those types of occasion, but if you want to take a more professional approach for the production of your short film, you should have some knowledge of the camcorder's manual functions too.

In this tutorial I will start by discussing three of the most basic functions: the focus, the iris and the zoom. The Focus control is usually the manual focus ring at the front of the lens, well certainly with professional cameras. It's a particularly useful function if used correctly. The ring turns anti-clockwise for a more distant focus and clockwise for a closer focus.

Next, I will talk about the Iris ring. This is also located on the lens. It manages how much light appears through the lens, through the adjustable opening called the aperture. As you let more light into the shot, it naturally becomes brighter.

Finally, I will talk about the zoom function. Many people use this function and it's often over used! Used in moderation, however, this very popular feature can be a really useful tool. This feature moves your perspective closer or further away from your chosen subject. I would advise however, that whilst shooting a long zoom, you use a tripod.

EXAM SKILLS

11 Remind students of the techniques already practised in the lesson.

Tapescript 63

So welcome to Film-maker's Club. I hope you're excited at the thought of making a film and that you're bursting with great ideas. I've put you all into groups, so here's what you're going to do. Now you might think the first thing that you need to do is to come up with an idea for a story, but even before that you need to think about what *type* of film you want to make.

Remember that a film is really a story in pictures. There are lots of ways of telling a story. So choose a style of film that suits the talents of the group. If you have talented artists, but no good writers, or actors, you might want to make your film in the style of a cartoon or some other kind of animation. Last year a group made an excellent film using Lego bricks.

So having decided that, you can start to think of your idea for the story. Think about the movies you like to watch. What is it that makes them interesting? Is it the characters, the plot? As regards plot, my advice is – don't be too ambitious, don't make it complicated. Keep it simple – the simplest ideas are often the ones that work the best. Initially you just need to find the basic concept. You can fill in the details later. It's a good idea to keep a notebook in your pocket and carry it everywhere. You never know when a great idea will suddenly come to you! And the more ideas, the better, in my opinion.

The next stage is to write the screenplay – for this you need to divide the story up into a series of scenes. For each scene, the screenplay should begin with a short description of where it takes place, the time of day, that is day or night. Then the rest consists of the script – the lines the actors will speak, and it should also describe the camera movements, and give directions to the actors about how they should move.

Before you can start filming, you need to prepare a storyboard of your film to help everyone involved to imagine the scenes clearly and to understand what you are trying to achieve. This is similar to a comic-book version of your film, but without speech balloons.

And at this point you need to appoint a director. This is a major role and it's vital that he or she is a good communicator, as they are the key link between the actors and the rest of the team. This person will have responsibility for the creative side of the project. He or she will have the final say in the choice of the main actors and in directing the action of the film.

That brings me to the next stage – casting your film – finding the actors. Don't just rely on your friends. Be creative! Perhaps you could advertise on social media. Or if your film needs a doctor, perhaps you could ask one from the local hospital if they could spare a couple of hours for you?

And then before filming finally starts, you will need to assign other jobs, such as director of photography – in your case this will be the person who operates the camera; someone in charge of sound and music, and someone in charge of costumes and props (including furniture and any other objects needed) and also someone to look after hair and make-up. But we'll look at these roles in more detail in our next session.

1 talents	2 simple	3 notebook
4 camera movements	5 comic book	6 creative
7 advertise		

SPEAKING

OUTCOMES

- discuss the topic of fame for Speaking Parts 2 and 3
- think about the different types of question you may be asked in Speaking Part 3
- use the appropriate tense when answering Part 3 questions.

OUTCOMES

In this lesson students expand their vocabulary on the topic of fame and the media. They practise Part 2 and learn more about how it relates to Part 3. There is a focus on both tenses and linking words.

LEAD-IN

01 If you prefer, bring in pictures of people from the students' country/countries who could be described by the adjectives.

Model the correct pronunciation of the words and get students to repeat them.

02 Read through the task card with the class. Students listen and answer the questions.

Extension

Students read the script and highlight introductory and linking phrases, and any other useful expressions such as 'I remember thinking…', 'finally'.

Tapescript 64

Well, for this task I'd like to talk about Bill Gates. He's the brilliant computer programmer who created Microsoft and the Windows operating system. I first saw Bill Gates on television in 2001. He was talking about Windows XP, which came out that year. I remember thinking that he is the richest man in the world, but if you look at him, you'd never know that. He just looks like a typical computer programmer.

I like Bill Gates because he's responsible for bringing computers to millions of family homes around the world with his Windows operating system. This made computers easier to use for everyone and also at a price that many families could afford. I also like him because he was the world's youngest self-made billionaire at the time. If he could do it, I like to think I could do it too. Finally, I admire him because he's very generous and uses his money to help people. He has given away a huge amount of his money to charity, and I believe he plans to give most of it away in the end. I think this is an excellent idea and I hope this can show other rich and powerful people that they should also help others.

1 Bill Gates	2 computer programmer
3 on television	4 2001, when Windows XP came out

5.1: He is responsible for bringing computers into family homes.

5.2: He was the world's youngest self-made billionaire.

5.3: He gives a lot of his money to charity.

03 Tell students that the words in the box are useful ways to link ideas and extend their talk. They listen and complete the gaps.

Alternative

Students try to fill in the gaps before listening. Then they listen and check.

Point out that 'in spite of' is followed by a noun (in this case 'his fame').

Tapescript 65

Well, the famous person I'm going to describe is David Beckham. He was a footballer who played for Manchester United, and he also played for England as well. I first saw him play for United when I was only seven, so that was probably in about 2002.
I remember it as one of the most exciting days in my life!

David Beckham became famous because he was a very talented footballer. His speciality was scoring amazing goals from free kicks. But he wasn't well-known only for his football skills. He became even more famous when he married a pop star – Victoria, one of the Spice Girls. And another reason for his fame was his good looks and his style. I think almost every boy in the world wanted to have a David Beckham haircut! I know I did.

I adored him as a boy because I was mad about football and he was my hero. The reason why I still like him is that in spite of his fame he behaves like a normal guy. I heard a story from someone whose car was broken down in the middle of the countryside. And then a car stopped and a man got out and asked him if he needed a push. It was David Beckham!

1 who	2 and	3 when	4 so
5 because	6 But	7 because/when	8 why
9 in spite of	10 whose		

04 Get students to complete the notes on a famous person in one minute. They do not have more than a few seconds to decide on the person. Quick decision-making is essential in Part 2.

05 Students work in pairs to do their own talks. Encourage them to put their own notes aside and listen to their partner, making notes of useful phrases or errors they hear.

Extension

To ensure students listen to their partner, have a follow up stage where each pair joins with another pair and talks about their partner's famous person.

06-07 The aim of exercises 06 and 07 is to familiarise students with the type of questions that are asked in Part 3. The important point to emphasise is that students will not be asked about their own experience in Part 3, but rather to do the functions exemplified in exercise 06 a to e.

The answers in exercise 07 are not limited to a few words. These are the minimum length of answer required. Even longer ones would be desirable.

Ask students to underline the verb forms. What tenses are used? Students need to listen carefully to the tenses and time phrases used in the questions to decide which tenses to use in their answers.

Extension

If you have a stronger class, you could ask them to add an example to each of the answers to extend them further.

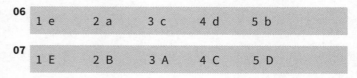

06				
1 e	2 a	3 c	4 d	5 b

07				
1 E	2 B	3 A	4 C	5 D

EXAM SKILLS

Students work with a partner to answer questions 1 to 6 in their own words. Ask them to cover up the answers given in exercise 7 or they may just read them out. Encourage them to extend their answers as much as possible.

Feedback

Circulate around the classroom while students are doing the activity. Note down any errors of tenses. If possible, record one or two students' answers and transcribe them for an error correction activity in the next class. Do this anonymously.

Ask students if their partners gave extended answers with specific examples.

UNIT / 08: NATURAL WORLD

READING

OUTCOMES

- complete notes with words from the text
- match sentence endings with their beginnings
- use modals of possibility and ability.

OUTCOMES

For all parts of the exam, it is important for students to have a good vocabulary connected to nature. Reading and listening texts often deal with some aspect of the natural world and there are Part 2 essays and speaking test tasks which deal with animals, their rights and how we treat them, as well as various environmental issues. The reading lesson provides practice of two task types. Both of these require students to use both meaning and grammatical clues to find the correct answers. The lesson introduces strategies to help with this. In language, the unit looks at two of the major functions of modals. Possibility helps students to express uncertainty, while ability enables them to talk about what they can and can't do.

LEAD-IN

01 Synonyms and antonyms are often used together in a sentence or paragraph as a form of cohesion. Each of these sentences contains either a pair or synonyms or a pair of antonyms. Students have to decide which. This exercise can also be used to work out meaning from context.

1 opposite	2 similar	3 similar
4 opposite	5 similar	

02 Students read the text in a minute to get the main points. Assign the pairs of words from exercise 01 to different students. They use the text to check whether the words are similar or opposite.

03 Read through the steps box and tip carefully with the students. The most important step is to make sure they are aware of where the words are coming from (the box or the text) and how many words they can use. They need to use grammar and meaning to work out what kind of words is needed in the gaps. They should consider prepositions, articles and other grammar words as clues, which can help them. Notes completion will be based on a section of the text so they have to locate the correct section and read it in detail.

Look at the example with the students. They should already be used to thinking of synonyms for key words.

04 This exercise gets students to focus on one paragraph and identify synonyms/paraphrase from that section of the text.

1 c	2 a	3 b	4 e	5 d

Extension

Prepare similar activities based on words/phrases in another paragraph. A stronger class may be able to make their own exercises in pairs and exchange them with another pair.

05 This exercise aims to raise awareness of the need to read only the relevant part of the text when completing a set of questions. Students often waste valuable time reading irrelevant parts of the text.

1 Hardy Jones	2 campaigner
The information was in paragraph B. No.	

06 Ask students to look at the gapped notes and quickly identify which paragraph they are based on. They can do this by identifying key words (orca, migrating, beluga, diver, icy, etc.). Read the first sentence of the notes together. Elicit the key words and synonyms from them. Point out that the gap follows 'a group of'. Ask what kind of word will fit. It will most likely be a type of sea creature, though they might suggest a group of people. Suggest that people would probably be in a boat and orcas don't usually attack humans. Encourage them to use their world knowledge, logic and common sense when answering reading questions.

1 grey whales	2 humpback whales	3 seven/7 hours
4 move her legs	5 leg	
The information was in paragraph E.		

07 Write the sentence beginning, 'Moko 'spoke' to the beached whales..' on the board. Go through the steps using that sentence beginning as an example. 'Beached' is probably a word the students are unfamiliar with. Sometimes it is possible to use existing knowledge to work out the meanings of unknown words. They know 'beach' and 'ed' endings are used when something is done to someone/thing (killed, hunted etc). Are whales supposed to be on the beach? (No) It should be clear that 'beached' means accidentally stuck on the beach'.

Get students to find the relevant part of the text (the end of Para D) as quickly as possible. Elicit what information has been covered in the sentence beginning (Moko...seemed to communicate with the whales). Ask what other information about Moko is in the text (...led them to a channel which took them back to the ocean). Ask students to complete the sentence beginning in their own words based on this information. Check whether the sentence completions they write make sense.

D

08-09 Students compare their own sentences with endings A, B and C, and say which one is most similar. Point out that C is wrong because it doesn't make sense logically. This exercise shows the importance of understanding connecting words like 'to' (purpose) and 'because' (reason). Refer students to the tip. If the exact words in the text are used, they could be a 'false friends'.

08

See exercise 9.

10 Remind students that there will be more sentence endings than beginnings. They will need to read the text carefully as several endings will fit grammatically and even in meaning if read without reference to the text.

When doing feedback, focus on any answers that students have got wrong. They need to understand what kind of error they have made (logical, not understanding a word in the text or question etc.). Careful analysis of their errors at this stage will help them next time they practise the same task type.

1 d	2 g	3 f	4 b	5 a

GRAMMAR FOCUS: MODALS OF POSSIBILITY AND ABILITY

11-12 Write the example sentence 'Experts think dolphins may understand that humans are similar to them.' on the board. Ask a student to come up and underline the modal. Ask what type of word follows the modal (infinite form of the verb). Ask 'Are experts sure that dolphins understand that humans are similar to them?' (No).

Draw students' attention to the second example. Ask them if 'can' and 'couldn't' are past or present'.

Extension

Students make their own sentences with 'may', 'might' 'could' for possibility and 'can', 'can't', 'could' and 'couldn't' for ability. Then have students share these with the class.

11

(in A) Dolphins' protection of humans might not be just automatic or instinctive: they may actively decide to help in certain situations.
(in F) Although we may never be sure why they help us…

12

they could tell, he couldn't get away

EXAM SKILLS

13 Students can do the practice task at home or timed in class. Allow about 20 minutes.

Alternative

If your class needs more support, start by asking them which zoos they've been to and what they think the purpose of zoos is, to get them to start thinking about the topic before reading. It is probably a good idea to let them do the questions alone so that you can see how individual students are coping.

1	entertainment	2	Gerald Durrell		
3	natural habitats	4	wild	5	enrichment
6	Webcams	7 H	8 G	9 D	10 E	11 A

WRITING

OUTCOMES

- deal with two-part questions
- link different parts of the essay
- write a conclusion.

OUTCOMES

Some Writing Part 2 questions have two parts to them and this lesson gives students practice at dealing with them. It also introduces some linking phrases, which provide 'signposts' to the reader to help them follow the essay. Students will learn what should and should not be included in the conclusion of their Part 2 essay.

LEAD-IN

01 Remind students that it is more useful to learn word pairs or short phrases. This exercise introduces some common collocations for describing the environment and its problems. Ask students which of the issues from the exercise they can see represented in the pictures.

1 d	2 c	3 f	4 e	5 b	6 a

Advice

Students are unlikely to learn a set of new words the first time they meet them. Come back to the words in the next lesson or a week later. Practise them in a variety of ways, such as games and quizzes to aid memorisation.

02 This exercise puts the word pairs they have learnt into context. It also introduces the kind of sentences that are suitable for the conclusion. Ask students how we know that these sentences belong in a conclusion (In conclusion, to sum up, finally, I suggest, etc.)

1	global warming	2	natural habitats
3	air pollution	4	endangered species
5	fossil fuels	6	renewable energy

03 Refer students to the tip. Tell them that in contrast to Part 1, where they just need a concluding sentence, Part 2 essays need a separate concluding paragraph composed of 3 or 4 sentences. They must organise themselves well to ensure they have time to write these.

In this exercise students learn that there are some guidelines to be followed for writing conclusions but also some options.

04 All of these example sentences are suitable for conclusions and can be matched with the features in exercise 03.

1 g	2 a	3 d	4 b	5 h	6 i

05 Read the essay question with the students. Remind them of the 4 options: Strongly agree, tend to agree, tend to disagree and strongly disagree. Ask them what their position is. Get them to note down a few ideas to support their point of view.

Tell them that a student who strongly agrees with the statement has written an essay on the topic. Elicit what they might include in the conclusion.

Students choose between paragraphs A and B. Get them to explain in their own words why the paragraph they have chosen is better.

Paragraph A is better because it includes the points in exercise 3. Paragraph B adds new information and supporting evidence, which are not appropriate for a conclusion, though B does also give the writer's opinion and answer to the question.

06 This exercise introduces useful linking phrases for Part 2 essays. All the phrases contain two or more words. Tell students that these phrases must be used exactly as they are. You usually can't miss out or change any of the words (e.g. *on other hand* or *on my view* are wrong).

1 f	2 d	3 g	4 a	5 e	6 b	7 c

07 This essay question has two parts to it. To make this clear, write the two parts on the board in separate columns:

Why has this happened?	What can governments do to stop this from continuing to happen?

Students write a few bullet points for each one.

Students come up to the board and note down their ideas.

08 Ask students to read the model answer and see if their ideas were mentioned. Point out that the essay structure is clear and simple:

Introduction

Answer first question

Answer second question

Conclusion

It is easy to complete the chart because the essay is well organised and it is easy to identify the main points.

Point out that the conclusion offers a summary of the main points but as they are presented in different words it doesn't seem like repetition.

Extension

Get students to highlight the linking words and expressions used in the essay. Are any of them repeated? (No) Can (stronger) students say what function they serve?

The causes	Government actions
habitats destroyed	education programmes
pollution	invest in clean energy

2 All of them are mentioned in the conclusion.

3 The conclusion ends with a *recommendation*.

GRAMMAR FOCUS: PRESENT PERFECT AND PAST SIMPLE

09-10 Make some statements in the present perfect, which relate to your current situation. Examples may include: the classroom door has been painted, Julia has had her hair cut or the weather has got colder. They should be things, which happened in the past but the effects are visible or felt now. Ask questions like 'When did Julia have her hair cut?' (Yesterday). Can we see it now? (Yes).

Students find the present perfect sentences from the essay. These activities began in the past and may be still going on. The results are all affecting the present.

09

2 Humans have destroyed their natural habitats.
3 Pollution has created problems for many sea creatures.

10

For example, the number of black rhinos has declined from over 65,000 in the 1960s to just 2,500 today.

EXAM SKILLS

11 Students work in small groups to brainstorm ideas for the essay topic and a possible structure for it.

Alternative

Half the class works on causes and the other on solutions. They can use their smart phones for research if they don't have enough ideas. Then encourage students to share their ideas whole class.

12 Students study the plan and compare it to their own ideas. This is probably the most obvious plan for the essay and it is also easy to follow.

Students write their essays individually in class or at home.

Sample answer

Global warming, also known as climate change, is the rising of temperatures all over the world because of human activity. In this essay I will explain the main causes of global warming and also suggest some solutions.

The earth's temperature is rising due to greenhouse gases, such as carbon dioxide, which get stuck in the air. One major cause is the increase in air pollution from burning fossil fuels like coal in factories and power stations. As the population grows, more energy is being used. Also, nowadays everyone owns several devices, such as computers, tablets and phones. These have to be charged every day. Another major problem is cutting down trees. Trees use carbon dioxide and release oxygen so we need a lot of them. People have cut down trees to use the wood for different purposes.

Although global warming is a major problem, there are some solutions. One of these is to use the. clean or renewable energy sources. For instance, solar power uses the sun to generate energy; we can also use the power of the wind and waves instead of fossil fuels. We need to protect the rainforests. For every tree that is cut down we need to plant a new tree. We can all help in different ways. One of them is to use public transport when possible and only have one car per family.

To sum up, humans have created the problem of global warming. Therefore, humans must also try to solve the problem. We can all try to live a 'green' lifestyle by saving electricity and not buying things we don't need. (268 words)

Feedback

In feedback, focus on the elements introduced in this lesson. In particular, give students credit for using the present perfect (or attempting to), for giving equal weight to the two parts of the question and using some of the linking expressions they have practised.

LISTENING

OUTCOMES

- listen to people talking about a topic related to work or study
- complete notes in a task
- use headings in the notes to guide you through what the speaker is saying
- use the speaker's 'signposting' words to help you follow notes.

OUTCOMES

This lesson develops students' ability to follow a talk by making use of the 'signposting' phrases the speaker uses as well as the notes themselves in the notes completion task.

LEAD-IN

01 Although students probably haven't heard of the specific types of animal, they will probably know the general type. They match up animal names and pictures. Ask them what they know about the animals or what they can see from the pictures.

| A | mountain gorilla | B | blue ring octopus |
| C | Pere David's deer | D | Arabian leopard |

02 Tell students that they won't hear the full name of the animal in the texts but will hear clues. Afterwards, ask them for the clues, which helped them find the answers.

Tapescript 66

Speaker 1

This creature is found in the mountains of Central Africa. It has black hair all over its body, which is much thicker than other members of the species. This means that it can live in colder temperatures. There are only about 900 of these apes in the wild. A lot of the green plants they eat have been destroyed, and they have also been killed in the past for their fur.

Speaker 2

This creature lives in the ocean from Australia up to Japan. Many of them are quite small, with a body that grows up to five centimetres long, and they have long tentacles, or arms. Its name comes from the bright blue rings that show up when it is frightened. You need to be careful in the sea around them as they are very poisonous.

Speaker 3

These creatures live mainly in desert areas and can survive in both mountains and valleys. Their tails help them to balance when they are climbing or sleeping in trees. Their black and yellow coats help them to hide in the places where they live. Unfortunately, there are only about 250 of these beautiful big cats left in the wild today.

Speaker 4

This strange looking animal lives in wet areas and comes from the area south of the tropics in China. There are very few in the wild now. As you can see, it has antlers like most deer, but it has a neck like a camel and hooves or feet like a cow. They eat mainly grass and live partly on land and partly in water.

| 1 mountain gorilla | 2 blue ring octopus |
| 3 Arabian leopard | 4 Pere David's deer |

03-04 These exercises help students link possible headings with notes and questions. 'Notes' signifies that the text may be bullet points and may not be written in full sentences. Point out that in exercise 4 some grammatical features are missing (e.g. subject pronouns are missing in notes b to e)

03

| 1 b | 2 e | 3 a | 4 c | 5 d |

04

| a 2 | b 3 | c 5 | d 4 |

05 Remind students (if appropriate) that they have used signposting expressions in their writing tasks. They are also a useful way to ensure they are following a talk in the listening test.

1 b	2 d	3 b	4 e	5 a	6 c

06-07 Tell students they should make use of the preparation time given before each set of questions to predict what kind of word they are listening for in each gap. They match gaps 1 to 5 with the type of word they are listening for.

07

2 a	3 d	4 b	5 c

08 Students will hear the passage about mountain gorillas twice. For the first listening, ask them to look back at exercise 05. They will listen for the signposting expressions and tick them when they hear them.

Tapescript 67

Hello everyone. Today I'm going to talk about a project I've done about the mountain gorilla. I think it's a truly fascinating animal. They originate in Africa – Central Africa, in fact.

So now I'm going to talk a little about where they live. As you can probably guess, and as you can see in this first photo, their name reflects the environment they live in – tropical mountain forests.

Now just like all other apes, they build nests out of leaves. But they don't make their nests high up as other species do – mountain gorillas make them on the ground instead. And they sleep wherever they end their day and they rarely sleep in the same bed twice!

So, I'll move on to talk about the physical features of the mountain gorilla. In other words, what it looks like. So here are some photographs on screen for you all to have a look at. This gorilla here on the left is a male gorilla. We know that he's an older male gorilla because of the colour of his coat. As you can see, his coat is grey. He's called a silverback. Younger male gorillas are called blackbacks. And there's an obvious reason for that! Yes, a young adult male has a black coat. As he gets older, his coat turns from black to grey.

Next, I'm now going to tell you a little about the diet of the mountain gorilla. Interestingly, mountain gorillas are herbivores. In other words, they survive on a diet of plants. As you can see from this next picture, this gorilla is eating leaves. And they also eat fruit and flowers. They occasionally eat insects too, but only when they're very hungry! And it might interest you to know that mountain gorillas very rarely drink water, even though they live in a very warm climate. It appears they get all the water they need from plants.

I'd like to conclude by talking about some of the threats that mountain gorillas face. They are in serious danger of disappearing from our world altogether. Let's have a look at two reasons why they're in such danger. And both of these reasons are connected to human activity. Firstly, people are damaging the mountain forests where these gorillas live. They're cutting down the trees to build farms and towns. Mountain gorillas live in close family groups and this means that it's difficult for them to get enough to eat in the small areas they now have to live in. Secondly, gorillas are also suffering as a result of hunting. Sadly, some people find and kill them to sell. So it's a very sad situation indeed for these beautiful animals.

09 Remind students that there may be several possible answers mentioned but only one will fit in the notes according to the meaning of the passage. Remind them that they should look at the heading as well as the gapped sentence. Tell them they can write either one or two words for each gap.

1 ground	2 grey	3 blackbacks / black backs
4 water	5 Hunting	

10 Ask students to look at the picture of the American bullfrog and try to describe it in pairs. Then ask them to share their ideas with the class.

Students read the notes and match the gaps to the questions.

Alternative

Students look at the notes and make their own questions before comparing with questions a to f.

1 d	2 a	3 c	4 b	5 e	6 f

11 Check students understand the instructions. They can write: just a word, just a number or a word and a number.

See if students can get the answers after just one listening. If not, play it a second time.

Transcript 68

Good morning, everyone. In today's lecture I want to talk to you about a very unpopular animal here in Britain. In fact, you could say that it's one of our least loved animals! It's called the American bullfrog and yes, it does in fact come from America – the east of America, to be exact – and it was brought to Britain in the early nineteenth century, so you could say that it's been here for quite a long time. It wasn't brought here on purpose– it actually arrived in a big container of aquatic plants. In other words, it was accidentally introduced into Britain!

Now, I'll tell you a little about its appearance. The American bullfrog is a very large – and ugly – species of frog. And when I say it's large, I mean *large*. Interestingly, female American bullfrogs are usually much larger than the males. In fact, they can weigh up to 750 grams, whereas the males only go up to about 600 grams. And take a look at its head – it's really broad and flat, isn't it? And you can see its mouth – just here – that's quite large too.

Now, both the male and the female American bullfrogs have green or brown bodies and have dark spots on the top. But there's one important difference between them – you can see that the male's throat is yellow but the female has a white one instead. And the other difference is their eardrums, here just behind their eyes. Those of the male are much larger than the female's.

So, let's move on to why we so dislike the American bullfrog. Well, this is because it has threatened our own native species of frogs. Firstly, it breeds very quickly indeed. For example, female bullfrogs can lay up to 25,000 eggs every single season. And secondly, the American bullfrog is very greedy. In fact, they eat just about anything they can put into their mouths! As well as other frogs, they eat insects, fish and have even been known to eat birds and snakes! So, in other words, they eat the food sources of our own native species. Thirdly, they carry a disease that is dangerous to other frogs. And finally, they don't just damage our natural world, they cause financial damage too. Around one hundred thousand pounds has been spent monitoring the American bullfrog in the wild.

So, as scientists, we can learn a lesson from this about the dangers of introducing any living species into a new environment.

1 19th / nineteenth	2 750 / seven hundred and fifty
3 head	4 yellow
5 snakes	6 100,000 / one hundred thousand

12 Tell students that it is important to proofread each section. They must spell words correctly and if a plural form is needed (like question 5), a singular form will be marked wrong. Advise students to write numbers as digits not words to avoid spelling mistakes.

EXAM SKILLS

13 Remind students to make use of preparation time to identify the type of information they are looking for. Tell them not to worry about any unknown words in the notes as they may not be necessary for completion of the task.

Transcript 69

OK everyone, I think we're ready to make a start. Now, when you think of a dangerous animal, what do you think of? A tiger perhaps? Or maybe a leopard? Most people think that all dangerous animals live on land, but in fact, some of the *most* dangerous animals on the planet live in our seas and oceans. I'm going to talk today about one of these – the box jellyfish.

There are different types of box jellyfish, and they are found in warm coastal seas anywhere from the Indian Ocean to as far north as Japan, but the most dangerous ones are found in the oceans around Australia.

OK, so now let's examine what these box jellyfish look like. There are no prizes for guessing why it's called a box jellyfish! You can see that it's shaped like a box or a cube, with four sides and rounded corners. And you can also see that its body is light blue.

So, let's take a look at the tentacles of the box jellyfish more closely. It's got fifteen of these growing from each of the four corners of the box. Now, you may be surprised to learn that these tentacles *can* grow to a length of *three metres*! And another surprising thing is its large number of eyes, that's six eyes on each of its four sides, so twenty-four altogether.

So now let's move on to talk about the sting of a box jellyfish. What is it? Well a jellyfish has a lot of tentacles, and each tentacle has thousands of cells which can produce a poison. If the tentacles come into contact with a fish, or a person, they stick to the their skin. If the tentacles are very long, they are in contact with a lot of the body, giving a bad sting which hurts terribly. This can be dangerous to the victim.

There are two ways that people can die as the result of a jellyfish sting. Firstly, a very severe sting can cause a person to have a heart attack. This can happen within minutes. Secondly, sometimes a swimmer goes into shock and can't make it back to the beach because they are in such extreme pain. If they're in the water alone, they'll die.

And now I'd like to conclude with advice on how to help someone who has been stung by a box jellyfish. If they have had a heart attack, of course the most important thing is to try to revive them first of all. And then, the best thing to help is vinegar. Yes, the same vinegar you use when you're cooking! Many Australian beaches keep bottles of it near the jellyfish warning signs. You should pour a bottle over the tentacles for 30 seconds, and then the tentacles can be removed. However, if you get stung and don't have any vinegar, you should pour seawater on the skin. This will help to ease the pain before you can get further medical help.

| 1 Australia | 2 3 / three | 3 24 / twenty-four |
| 4 stick | 5 pain | 6 (sea) water |

SPEAKING

OUTCOMES

- extend your knowledge of vocabulary related to animals and their habitat
- talk at length about animals and pets for Speaking Parts 2 and 3
- develop your answers in Part 3.

OUTCOMES

The speaking lesson of this unit extends the topic of animals and pets and helps students further develop their vocabulary. They will practise parts 2 and 3, learning how to give longer answers to part 3 questions.

LEAD-IN

01 Ask students to look at the pictures and match them to the animals. They choose a characteristic and a habitat for each one.

| A eagle: big claws, nest |
| B dolphin: long fin, underwater |
| C camel: round hump, desert |
| D deer: hard antlers, forest |

02 Students work in groups of 4. Each describes one of the animals. Allow them to use dictionaries to find additional words if needed.

03 Read through the task card with the students. Check meanings of the words in the box.

Students complete the notes. Remind them they normally have one minute for this.

04 Students take it in turns to do their task in front of a partner. They can record themselves on their smart phones if they wish, in order to review and improve their performance. Tell students that they need to listen to their partner in order to ask a question about the animal (something that hasn't been covered in the talk).

Extension

If students are willing, one or two can give their talk to the class. Don't' force them to do this but praise them for having a go.

05 Remind students that part 3 will challenge their thinking skills as well as their English. They will be asked to give reasons, explanations, recommendations etc. Exercise 05 gives examples of some questions that may be asked on the topic of the natural world and some good ways for students to start their answers.

Refer them to the first tip and remind them that they are marked on the range of their vocabulary and grammar so they should avoid repeating phrases like 'I think'.

Tell students that when listening for the key words in the examiner's question, they should remember that in English, words that carry meaning are stressed.

Transcript 70

1

| **Examiner:** | What can governments do to prevent illegal hunting? |
| **Student 1:** | There are two things the government can do to prevent illegal hunting. The first is to be more serious about punishing hunters, for example … |

2

| **Examiner:** | Should the government provide more money for zoos? |
| **Student 2:** | They definitely should. It seems to me that zoos need money now more than ever. Many of them have very old facilities for the animals … |

3

| **Examiner:** | How might we be able to protect wildlife in the future? |
| **Student 3:** | Well, in the future, it might be a good idea to use technology to track where wild animals are … |

4

| **Examiner:** | Is there any difference in how children learn about wildlife now than in the past? |
| **Student 4:** | There's a big difference, I think. In the past, we used to go on more field trips to places to see wild animals, but now we mostly just see them on the internet. |

| 1 b | 2 a | 3 d | 4 c |

06 Remind students that they are likely to need to use past, present and future tenses in part 3. In this set of questions they need to use all three.

Go around the class and monitor students' responses. If you hear a particularly good answer, invite the student to share it with the class at the end.

07 It is important for students to provide extended answers in part 3. This exercise provides suggestions of how to extend answers by giving examples or reasons. Remind students that they should be regularly reading and listening to documentaries and news programmes both in English and their own language so that they have enough to say about the topics that feature in IELTS.

Students listen and complete the table.

Transcript 71

| **Examiner:** | What should be done to people caught hunting illegally? |
| **Student:** | Well, if you ask me, I think people caught hunting should pay all the money they made |

to charities that help to protect animals. And the same for people caught buying these animal products. For example, I read that the government in Kenya took money from people who were caught buying animals' furs. The reason why is that it will help charities better protect wild animals, and hopefully make hunting more difficult.

2

Examiner: Is there anything we as individuals can do to prevent hunting?

Student: Yes, there are many things we can do, and perhaps the most important one is to stop buying things made from animals. A good reason for this is that it might cause the demand for things made from animals to drop. For instance, many of the world's most famous fashion designers have stopped using real animal fur in their clothes.

3

Examiner: Will there be more or less hunting in the future?

Student: In my opinion, there will be less hunting in the future. The reason for this is that many of our animals are already close to becoming extinct, so when they are gone, there will be nothing left to hunt. By way of example, the white rhino in Africa was hunted for many years, but now there are almost no white rhinos left to hunt.

---

1 **Question:** What should be done to people caught hunting illegally?

Answer: They should have their money given to animal charities and the same for people buying the animal products.

Example: The government in Kenya took money from people were caught buying animal furs.

Reason: This will help those charities better protect wild animals

2 **Question:** Is there anything we as individuals can do to prevent hunting?

Answer: We can stop buying things made from animals.

Example: Most fashion designers no longer use real fur, they use fake fur instead.

Reason: The demand for things made from animals with drop, and so will demand for hunting.

3 **Question:** Will there be more or less hunting in the future?

Answer: I think there will be less hunting in the future.

Reason: Many of our animals are already close to becoming extinct.

Example: There are almost no white rhinos left.

---

08 Ask students to copy the table into their exercise books with the column headings but without the questions. Ask students for their suggestions for possible part 3 questions related to the general topic of the natural world. Help them if necessary. Possible questions include:

How can we as individuals help protect the environment?

What can governments do to slow down global warming?

Do animals now have more rights than they did in the past?

They make their own table with examples and reasons.

Students ask and answer questions using their completed tables to help them.

09-10 These exercises prepare students for the exam skills task by providing some ideas for them to answer the questions.

Suggested answers				
Pets:	1 C	2 B	3 A	4 D
Zoos:	1 G	2 F	3 E	4 H

EXAM SKILLS

11 Working in pairs, one student asks the questions on pets while the other answers. They change roles for the set of questions on zoos. Remind them to include personal examples of their own or their friends' pets or their own visits to zoos.

Alternative

So that students can practise answering on both topics they alternate questions.

Feedback

As you go around the classroom, encourage students to extend their answers, listen out for examples and reasons given and invite individual students to share good answers with the class at the end.